The Dream is Over

London in the 60's, heroin,
and John and Yoko

The Dream is Over

London in the 60's, heroin,
and John and Yoko

DAN RICHTER

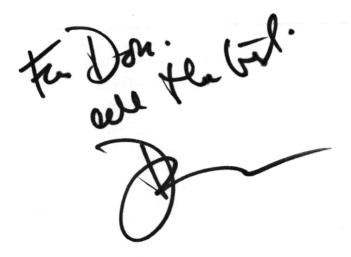

QUARTET

First published in 2012 by
Quartet Books Limited
A member of the Namara Group
27 Goodge Street, London W1T 2LD

A catalogue record for this book
is available from the British Library

ISBN   978 0 7043 7277 1

Typeset by Antony Gray
Printed and bound in Great Britain by
T J International Ltd, Padstow, Cornwall

1

Contents

Foreword: Yoko Ono 9

Introduction 11

A Leave of Absence 15

Don't Think Twice, It's All Right 20

The Princess and the Poet 23

A Slow Boat to Tokyo 31

You Can't Go Home Again 38

In London Hip is Becoming Cool 43

A Telegram to Chairman Mao 49

David 57

Yoko Ono Comes to Town 61

Hanover Gate Mansions 64

John becomes Yoko's Patron 70

Yoko and Ornette Coleman at the Albert Hall 73

Yoko Brings John to Tea 77

Things Start to Get Heavy 80

Christ, You Know It Ain't Easy 84

It's Only Rock 'n' Roll 95

Hare Krishna, Hare Rama 102

Cold Turkey 112

A Working Class Hero 121

Fly and Up Your Legs Forever 125

Power to the People 134

Don't Worry, Kyoko   141

Back to Work at Ascot   148

Politics, Oz, Warhol, and Dylan   152

Mr Buckley, I Presume?   159

Cannes – The Fortnight of the Directors   163

Recording Imagine   169

Filming Imagine   176

A Custody Trial in St Thomas   180

The Concert for Bangladesh   183

Some Time in New York City   186

Ten for Two and Attica at the Apollo   193

Changes   199

Michael X – The Murders in Trinidad   202

Cannes, Ringo, and George   205

Ladies and Gentlemen, the Rolling Stones   207

The One to One Concerts   210

A Spanish Vacation and a Shoot-out in Huston 214

Yoko Invests in Me (and *Cain's Book*)   218

Dear John   223

Across the Universe   225

My Passport Stamps (1969–73)   230

Acknowledgements   234

Foreword: Yoko Ono

When I think of the 60's, Dan & Jill Richter first come to mind. Dan will be wearing a red shirt with a bright yellow tie, green velvet pants and a black hat to match his dark grandma glasses, usually sitting in their large Victorian living room, just ruminating. I will never forget the first time I met Jill. She was sitting at the window, looking over the street, wearing a shimmering dark purple long dress, and white lace half-gloves which revealed her beautiful fingers. It's not an exaggeration to say that they impressed me as the epitome of the elegant London of the sixties. There was a large bowl of cash sitting on a elaborately carved wooden table, and people who visited them- film-makers, poets and writers - took the cash when they were ready to leave after a few smokes.

Dan told me that he didn't want friends to have to ask him for cash, so he just had it in the bowl for them to take. He was crazy like that. Jill, on the other hand, was not easy for people to get to know. As with most beautiful women, people just appreciated her physical beauty, not realising the incredible strong spirit hiding underneath it.

Neither of them were able to write about us quickly like the other writers did right after John's death. Now Dan has written his memories. Well, good for him. It's better that he lets his memories be carved in words, if not in stone . . . yoko

For Tom

Introduction

'Was this before you met John Lennon?'

My son Will was helping me sort and index my old papers for this book. He had found a group of faded photographs from a winter I spent in India. The pictures were of me with my friends Princess Zina Rachevsky, Ron Vial, Sacha Jung, and Peter Bendrey.

'Yeah, by a couple of years . . . '

'You guys look so stoned and happy. Where was this?'

'It's Srinagar in Kashmir. It was the spring 1964 just before I first met Yoko in Tokyo. Yeah we were stoned and happy, very happy.'

Taking the pictures from Will, the memories stirred old feelings. There I was sitting cross-legged on the carved wood fantail of our houseboat 'Soul Kiss', painting with inks in my notebook. In another picture Ron, Sacha, Zina, Peter and I were clowning around on the wall of the Shankaracharya temple high above Srinagar. In a third, Zina and I were sitting in a little gondola-like boat called a *shikara*, a robe across our legs. In her hair Zina wore a garland of daisies I had woven. The pictures were fading but like the youth on Keats' *Grecian Urn*, we were frozen in time, forever young, forever happy, forever on a spiritual quest. I can still see the faces, hear the words, and experience the feelings. It was the Sixties, the circles I travelled in were redolent with grass but gradually the cold hands of harder drugs touched everything I did.

This memoir starts in 1963 when I gave up my secure life as lead performer and teacher at the American Mime Theatre in New York. I set out on a journey that began as a year's leave of absence but turned into a ten-year odyssey that took me around the world. By the time I returned to the Mime Theatre, I had published two volumes of *Residu*, a beat poetry review, become a heroin addict, starred in Stanley Kubrick's *2001: A Space Odyssey*, and lived and worked with John Lennon and Yoko Ono.

The years I spent with John and Yoko were the culmination of my journey exploring the new hip life style. I was caught up in the cultural sea change that so many of us experienced during the Sixties. I have only briefly touched on the period I worked with Stanley Kubrick since it has been covered in detail in my book *Moonwatcher's Memoir*. My time in India, Japan, Athens and London I have described in more detail. My experiments with drugs and expanded consciousness parallel what many of my contemporaries went through in London at that time.

As I began my journey, across the ocean the Beatles were about to become voices that, like the Pied Piper of Hamelin, would call the youth around the world to join us on our wild and exhilarating journey. The world was changing as fast as my consciousness was expanding. The jazz and classical music I listened to was soon going to be submerged in a sea of rock and roll.

I met John when he and Yoko fell in love. I lived with Yoko and John from 1969 to 1973. I was Dan, Yoko's 'American friend,' who came along for the ride; a co-conspirator, confidant, assistant, and dope buddy; I was an insider who witnessed the break-up of the Beatles, John and Yoko in love, and John's transition from being a major rock star to the hagiographic status that he holds today. I was there from the first days at Tittenhurst Park in Ascot where we recorded *Imagine*, to the political days in New York, and then their retreat into that castle of an apartment house on Central Park West, 'The Dakota.'

I have tried to tell my story as I lived it. The sections dealing with John and Yoko were difficult to write since so much has already been written about them. To me they were good friends and I have tried to describe the life we were living then; how we talked, what we did.

Introduction

I can still see the vivid cast of people that surrounded them. There were stars, charlatans, groupies, politicians, sycophants, cops, reporters, lawyers, and hippies. These were exciting and tumultuous years. It was a time of absolute freedom, a time when everything changed. The world was turning on, tuning in, and dropping out and all to the beat of rock and roll. I had a unique view of this period in rock history. But my story is also more personal than that. I can really only tell you what happened to me: how, with their help, I finally kicked heroin, how my dreams and aspirations were almost fulfilled just to break once again like a wave on the shore of alcoholism and drug addiction.

Infinite slow motion – white feet slide on the cypress floor.
A hand slowly rises to a head bowed in sorrow . . .
Two ghosts weep for their lost poet lover.

DAN RICHTER
Kanze Kaikan Noh Theatre
Tokyo, May 13, 1964

A Leave of Absence

'Danny the Mime Theatre is going to miss you.'

Paul J. Curtis had his back to me and was looking sombrely out of the window of his office at the American Mime Theatre on Lower 3rd Ave in New York. Paul was pissed at me and struggling to contain his emotions. When he turned to look at me his dark eyes bore right through me. I loved Paul; he had taken me from a gangly young acting student and honed me into the lead performer of his Mime Theatre. I could see a hint of sadness hiding behind his stern exterior.

'I've made up my mind, Paul. I'm taking a year's leave of absence – I'm going to study mimetic forms in theatres around the world.' I added, to assuage him.

'It's not that simple Danny,' he said. 'We have to cast and retrain someone to do all your parts in the repertory. I have to find someone to take on your classes at the American Academy and the Jean Frankel theatre workshop. If you return in a year I can't guarantee you'd be able to step right back in. This is a serious decision you're making; serious for you and serious for the Mime Theatre.'

Paul always made me squirm. He was of medium height with a hard disciplined body from years of performing and he had a strong and forceful personality. After studying with Lee Strasberg and the German director Irwin Piscator at the New School for Social Research, he spent a number of years working as a performer on French television where he was exposed to French mime techniques. With an iron will, talent, and a touch of genius, this tough little man had hammered out a new performing medium based on traditional mime techniques and the method acting he had learned from Lee Strasberg.

I steeled myself and looked right into his piercing eyes. 'Paul I've really made up my mind. This isn't a casual decision, I'm taking the leave.'

There was a long pause as Paul looked back at me and then without even so much as a blink he sat down at his antique wooden desk and reached for his address book. 'Well then Danny,' he said, 'we'll have to call Ruth Mayles at the American National Theatre Academy. You'll need a decent set of papers to facilitate introductions to the theatres you'll want to visit.'

A wave of relief washed over me. I had done it; the prospect of the year ahead excited and scared me. I had no way of knowing it would last for ten.

At twenty-three I was skinny with blue eyes and dark curly hair. I knew I had an exceptional gift as a performer and teacher, but felt there was something missing. Like many of my generation who were born into the chaos of the Second World War, I was caught up in the smoky restlessness of the early sixties in New York.

My father, Mischa Richter, was a successful New Yorker cartoonist. My mother Helen was a young actress from Connecticut. They had met in New York and fallen in love. My early years were spent comfortably in Darien. Our friends were the successful writers and artists who lived in Connecticut to be close to New York. My life was secure and easy. I went to a little private school called Plumfield with other well-off children.

The seeds of addiction were planted early. As long as I can remember I have had migraine headaches.

My parents felt that a visit to a psychiatrist might help. I remember sitting on his carpet with an array of dolls in front of me and being asked questions like. 'What is the daddy doll doing to the mommy doll?' The upshot of all this was my being prescribed a tranquilliser called Miltown, now known as Meprobamate. Miltown is now known to be habit forming. I would use it in ever increasing doses for years.

Our lives changed with the start of the McCarthy era. My parents were targeted as left-wing intellectuals and decided to spend a year in Europe during 1950 and 1951. I was well ahead in my schooling so during our stay abroad, they did not send me to school. I spent most of my time in museums and visiting cultural sites with my family.

On our return to the States, I was sent off to Kent, a prep school in Northwestern Connecticut. It was a difficult adjustment. I was expected to attend the daily Episcopal Church services and there I heard the word 'kike' for the first time.

At Kent, as well as taking my Miltown, I began drinking and using Benzedrine and Dexedrine to help me study. I was a bad drunk and during my senior year left for a stay at the Menninger Clinic in Topeka, Kansas. I am not sure it helped, but after a couple starring roles at the Topeka Civic Theatre I realised I had a gift for performing and loved it. After a year as an outpatient at Menninger's, I joined my family for a year in Rome and then returned to New York to pursue an acting career. While at the American Academy I met Paul Curtis and joined the American Mime Theatre.

I began some tentative experiments in consciousness expansion. Now and then I would smoke marijuana with friends, and twice I tried the peyote buttons that Huxley described in *The Doors of Perception.* I bought them from a quirky little shop down on the Lower East side. This was the closest I could get to mescaline that Huxley wrote about. The visionary experiences I had on these first trips shattered my comfortable world. This was so different from the dull weight of Miltown and the other tranquillisers the doctors had prescribed me, it was like the coming of sound and colour to the movies. The yearnings I had felt that there must be something more to life, some meaning I wasn't getting, were suddenly justified. Being high on peyote and pot, seemed to fill a vast inner void and I found myself looking through a portal into a strange and promising world that I could not resist.

I read Allen Ginsberg's *Howl* and William Burroughs's *Naked Lunch.* I began to believe that drugs were just misunderstood. White uptight Christian culture used alcohol while the intuitive black culture used drugs. I saw them as a conduit for feelings, intuition, creativity, visions, and believed they would help me get in touch with my natural self, the God within.

The Cuban Missile Crisis in October of 1962 had shaken us all to the core. Living through those days on the brink of a global nuclear war left me disillusioned and stunned. During that winter and spring my plan to take a leave of absence from the American Mime Theatre was hatched. I wanted to spend a year hitch-hiking around the world like the Beats I had read about. I wasn't just going to read about being totally free, I was going to live it. I had told Paul Curtis that my purpose was to research different forms of mime, but my true agenda was to follow the trail of Allen Ginsberg and the other Beats. Like those I wished to emulate, I would set off with little money and the intention of staying high as much as possible. I was going to travel the world and experience whatever life had to offer.

On arriving in Europe I went first to East Berlin and spent two weeks at the Berliner Ensemble, Bertolt Brecht's theatre. Brecht had died a few years before, but his wife Helene Weigel was continuing his work. I was able to watch the plays in rehearsal and then in performance. I moved on to Paris to study the works of mimes like Jacques Lecoq and spent time at the *Comédie-Française.* I found a free place to stay above *Le Mistral* Bookshop. George Whitman, the owner, would let writers sleep in the upstairs rooms for free. There I found others like me who wanted to break loose from the confines of our restrictive society. At night we would smoke grass and talk about freedom and the visions we had when we were high.

On the evening of Friday November 22 I was walking in Paris with a new friend, Erik Swartz, and two girls. We had just had supper and were hoping for romance. Walking back to Erik's little hotel, *La Reine Blanche* on the Left Bank, we heard the news of the assassination.

'*Kennedy est mort! Oui, à Dallas. Il est assinee.*' You could see the stunned looks on people's faces as they talked excitedly in the streets.

We talked all night sitting in Erik's cramped little hotel room. It was then I decided to hitch-hike to India in the morning. That had been my plan since I arrived in Europe six weeks earlier. I didn't want to wait any longer. Erik decided to join me. We grabbed our few belongings and rode the Metro to the end of the line. We found ourselves at the *Autoroute du Sud,* the main artery that runs south from Paris toward Italy and beyond, with thousands of miles ahead of us. It was November 23rd, 1963. I had about $150 and a passport in the inside pocket of my jacket. The Beatles *Please Me* LP had been number 1 in the British charts for the 29th week. In Tokyo, Yoko Ono's daughter, Kyoko, was just three and a half month's old.

Erik and I had our thumbs out. It was cold, windy and clear after a night of heavy rain. We looked scruffy and wild-eyed with long hair and slept-in clothes. We shivered as we stood on the wet pavement with our collars up against the chill wind that was blowing from the north. You could smell the wet leaves on the ground. A trucker stopped his big *camion* and shouted down from his cab, '*Ou allez vous?*'

'*A l'Inde,*' to India I shouted back over the noise of the engine.

'*Zut!*' The Gauloise he was puffing on almost fell out of his lips. Then a smile crossed his craggy face. '*Alors, allons.*' He opened the door and motioned us up to the cab. We jumped in and threw our small knapsacks behind the seat. Our long overland journey to India had begun.

Don't Think Twice, It's All Right

'I bet Allen Ginsberg didn't have to stand in the rain getting soaked when he went to India,' I said as we stood by the road in the rain. The truck driver who had picked us up outside of Paris had dropped us off somewhere near Lyons in the middle of France.

'He probably took a plane,' muttered Erik as he raised his collar.

Our quest had rapidly turned into a soggy ordeal. The rain kept falling and between rides our clothes became saturated. Our next ride was with a young German kid who had run away from home in his little VW Beetle. Having nothing better to do, he announced that he would drive us to India. On the road between Venice and Trieste I fell asleep on the back seat. I was awoken violently when the Beetle skidded on the rain-soaked pavement, flew off the road and landed in a ditch. The car was probably totalled and we were all shaken up but unhurt. While our new friend was talking to the police, Eric and I put out our thumbs and caught another ride.

'I have to hear Bob Dylan's *Don't Think Twice, It's All Right*, I said to Eric as we sat beside a road in Northern Greece. The sun was finally starting to come out and Dylan's song seemed to exactly fit how I felt. I was leaving it all behind.

'Well it's not a long and dusty road,' quipped Eric, 'it's more like long and soggy.'

'If I bought you a guitar could you play it?' I asked. Eric was pretty good on the guitar and I had heard him play some Dylan songs in Paris.

'Yeah I know it. You're nuts Dan, you've only got about a hundred dollars on you.'

'I gotta hear it man! I bet I can find one and some new boots as well, better than these soggy ones I'm wearing.'

In a little village I found a small guitar, a pair of boots, dry socks and I even had a few dollars left.

For the next two days Eric played *Don't Think Twice* and lots of other songs, and my feet were warm and dry.

The trip took many weeks and was long and hard. In Baghdad, holed up in the YMCA, we survived the street fighting that followed the takeover of the government on November 18 by Abdul Arif. In Northern Iran we waited out a snow storm in the holy city of Meshad on the Afghani and Russian borders. After a week snowed in we finally were able to cross the frozen passes to the south and crossed the Baluchi desert into Quetta in Pakistan. All the time my consciousness was changing. I had brought a small piece of hash from Paris. It was dangerous to smoke it as we travelled. I had to mix a bit with tobacco and find a dark and lonely spot where no one could see me or smell the hash, then go back to our room to be high. I would squeeze my eyes closed and watch the mandalas spin in my head – aching to see more. 'Is this what the yogis see when they meditate?' I thought.

As I sat in our dimly lit room in a hostel or an Arab hotel and the visions filled my head, I felt a communion with all the other Beats and travellers everywhere that were high too. We really were a new generation sharing the gift of expanded consciousness. Just as the Buddhists had learned that freeing the mind had to be for all sentient beings and not just for personal liberation, we knew our dreams and visions were not just for ourselves but for a new world without war, racial prejudice, and class divisions.

What struck me most about drug use was the complete shift of consciousness I went through each time I got high. At first there would be those moments of anticipation before the high came on and then there it would be, everything would change; sights, smells, feelings, but most of all perception itself. It was as if I had been living in a well-ordered black and white movie and suddenly everything was in colour and unpredictable.

'What happened to the hash?' Eric asked as we sat in the Baghdad YMCA, waiting out the fire fight taking place on the streets outside.

'It's gone, we smoked it,' I said.

My dreams would have to wait until we reached India.

The Princess and the Poet

Princess Zina Rachevsky swept into the American Express offices on Connaught Circus, in the centre of New Delhi. She was over six feet, with long blond hair, and her fire engine red sari flowed as she moved purposely toward Ron Vial and I.

'You must be Ron Vial. Allen said you were tall. He also said you were very cool, a good source of dope, and a poet.'

As she turned towards me, I fell impossibly in love. 'And you're Dan, the mad poet who just hitch-hiked here from Paris. I'm Zina, Zina Rachevsky.'

She had a nervous little brown Yorkie in her arms and looked absolutely fantastic in her sari, gold, jewelled chains, and high Russian boots. Allen Ginsberg had been in Delhi the year before and had met Ronnie and written to Zina about him. Ronnie had been teaching at the American School in Delhi. Before that, he was in Dharmsala and Dalhousie in the Indian hill country, teaching English to the incarnate Tibetan Lamas. They were children chosen at birth as reincarnations of past lamas and had been brought out of Tibet with the Dalai Lama in exile. Ronnie was tall, urbane, and terribly cool. I had run into him at the Delhi YMCA, a hang-out for the hip young kids who were descending on India. Allen Ginsberg was our pied piper, writing about his travels, singing of freedom. Ragged, footloose, and impecunious, we were arriving in India with our heads bursting with dreams of giving up the world and getting high.

'The Maharaja of Kashmir has found me a houseboat on Dal Lake in Srinagar,' Zina went on. 'He's such a lovely man; I think he's in love with me.'

She tossed her golden hair. 'I'm spending the winter there. The houseboat is all carved wood with rugs and hangings, sort of Victorian Kashmiri.'

'Sounds great,' Ronnie said.

'Why don't you all come and join me? It has two bedrooms, dining room, living room, and a porch over the water. Servants too. My son Alex and I can share the main bedroom and you guys can use the second.'

A week later Ronnie and I were on a bustling crowded train creeping north in fits and starts to Pathankot in the foothills of the Himalayas. In Pathankot I saw my first Tibetan refugees, an old man and a young boy. The old man wore colourful robes, had a stringy beard, and looked like a wizard. Ronnie said hello to them in Tibetan and pulled out his wallet to show them a picture of the Dalai Lama. They immediately put their hands together and bowed their heads to the ground. As we walked away Ronnie said: 'They have to keep their heads lower than His Holiness, that's why they bowed so low.'

We were supposed to meet Ron's friend, Sacha Jung, at the bus station but he had not showed up. We waited a day and he didn't arrive, we got on a bus and took a hair-raising two-day ride over the Banihal Pass.

We stopped overnight in a tiny hamlet below the summit of the pass.

'Why are there so many wrecks of buses and trucks in the gorge below?' I asked the turbaned Sikh bus driver. We were in a tiny tea-house, sitting by a fire, with a clear local brandy, and a pipe of hashish. Around us, hill people were walking barefoot in the freezing mud and patches of snow.

'Well Sahib, as you have observed, we go over the Banihal Pass in a convoy. The road is always collapsing. When there are land slides and avalanches, they must work continually to keep just one lane open. If a new convoy is ready, we all go in one direction and when we have crossed, the next convoy moves over the pass in the opposite direction. If a bus or truck breaks down and can't be fixed, we must push it over the side so the convoy may pass.'

We had to constantly stop for the dirt and gravel road to be cleared of debris and re-cut where sections had fallen away. Ronnie and I huddled, freezing in the back of the bus. On the afternoon of the second day you can imagine the relief we felt as we descended into the Vale of Kashmir with its saffron fields and almond orchards sleeping under the cold pall of winter. Before dark we entered the ancient city of Srinagar which sits among lakes and canals, a jewel in the centre of the valley surrounded by snow-capped mountains. To the North are the great peaks of the Karakorum, crowned by Nanga Parbat, the ninth highest peak in the world.

From the bus station we took a gaudily painted *tanka*, a horse carriage, to the Dal Gate, a wide canal that leads into Dal Lake. Zina's ornate houseboat, Soul Kiss, was moored on the far side of the canal. She was standing on the porch dressed in a pink pheran, the ubiquitous short Kasmiri robe worn in the winter. We called across and Zina waved and sent Habib Tula, the owner of Soul Kiss, to paddle one of the little skiffs they call a *shikara* across to pick us up. The houseboat was a delight of carved lattice and hard wood. Kasmiri rugs and hangings covered the walls. Through the window we could see views of Dal Lake surrounded by tall chinar trees. On every side, great peaks rose to dizzying heights.

'Welcome sahibs, welcome to Soul Kiss,' Habiba said as he helped us with our bags. 'Shall I prepare tea, M'm Sahib?'

'Absolutely, we'll have it in the living room.' Zina replied. We followed her into the living room, the yorkie running ahead of us.

While Habiba and his family prepared tea, Zina told us about all the local saints and holy men she was planning to visit.

'Well, I for one could use a joint,' said Ronnie as he collapsed on the couch. 'I hope Mr Tula won't mind.'

'Oh don't worry about Habib, he's very accommodating,' she said.

Out the window I could see the Western Himalayas and as I smoked the potent hashish, I felt my soul exploding out and up to the distant glaciers.

A day later Sacha arrived. Sacha was a long bearded stocky Bavarian iconoclast – a hip guru who had attained his hipness while living in a tiny attic garret in the legendary Beat Hotel on Rue Git-le-Coeur in Paris. He had an impish light in his eyes, always lived in the moment, and was my first real introduction to terminal hipness. I spent many long hours talking with him about my dilemma. I was being inexorably drawn by the hip life style and was weighing giving up my mime career.

'I don't think I can go back to the life of a New York mime teacher and performer. At best, I'll be a male Martha Graham going to uptown cocktails parties flattering the rich who sit on the boards of foundations that fund the arts.'

'You gotta live in the moment baby. If you just let it happen, it'll be what it should be.'

'The problem is that I don't know where I'm going yet.'

My journals had begun to fill with poetry and painting and I had a sense that a lot of it was really pretty good. It seemed to be an outgrowth of this new life I was living.

'If I take this dizzying step into the void I will leave behind the security of being a successful performer and teacher. Poets don't make any money and most artists just starve. I'll be just another out-of-work beatnik.'

'Hey Baby, you can't be anything but free.' Sacha passed me a red clay chillum filled with the deeply redolent black hashish of the area. 'You don't know the future baby, no one does. Just be real, let it happen. It will anyway.'

I was hallucinating Yehudi Menuhin, George Malcolm, and Ambrose Bierce building incredible structures from a Bach Sonata in the vivid spring air. Was this a real search for freedom or was it the fibrous little roots of nascent drug addiction insinuating themselves in my soul?

I sat there, stoned out of my mind, with visions filling my head. I was trying to capture them with the poetry and paintings I was creating. I wanted to represent the changes so many of us were going through. Wings were growing on my naked body. Tangible visions were swirling above my head.

Drugs had become a major part of my life. We all believed that we were expanding our consciousness and reaching levels of perception and understanding that could only be attained through getting high or the rigours of meditation and spiritual disciplines.

When I turned on I could feel something snap, a change that was overwhelming as I tumbled forward into sensory overload. I know now that it was the seeds of addiction that were pulling so hard on me. Feelings long repressed were emerging under the cover of the rush created as dopamine overwhelmed my brain cell receptors.

Life on the houseboat was indeed idyllic. We painted and wrote poetry, smoked hashish and opium. And we talked. We talked about our lives, the hip thing, music, and the spiritual life.

On cold days Habiba would give us a *kangri*, a little clay pot in a wicker basket. He would fill it with hot embers. Kasmiris carry them under their loose pherans or put them beside them to keep warm. We would go into Srinagar in a *shikara* on the canals. The Muslim-Hindu crisis had the people on edge. One day on our way into town kids threw stones at us as we paddled by. Ronnie was hit in the forehead and bled all over the cushions.

Spring seemed to arrive quickly and soon blossoms were everywhere. Little candy-striped tulips popped up wherever we looked, even on some of the old sod-covered roofs.

Across the canal one morning, Peter Bendry arrived riding a bicycle. Very young, pretty hip but still ingenuous, Peter was already a traveller. He brought youth to our cabal.

We began visits to holy people. Behind a nearby Lakshmi temple we met toothless old Somaji who had meditated so long in the high mountain snows that frostbite had taken his fingers and toes. He was wrapped in an old army blanket held together with a big safety pin. He sang mantras and smoked hash in a Bombay hookah made from a coconut and was cared for by a little dark Nepali woman. Behind the same temple we met a holy woman whose ceiling had thousands of dried flowers hanging from it. She showed us a picture of Jesus on the cross and asked us why Westerners came to India to find God when we had a perfectly good one already? 'Did you see those spaced out little girls taking care of her? I'm sure she's a witch,' Zina said, as we walked back down the hill to our *tanka*.

Lasa Baba was a young Muslim holy man who drew great crowds of devotees. We were planning a trip to see him one afternoon when there was a bustle from the back of the boat where Habib and his family stayed. Habib scurried into the living room, picked up some of the best cushions and put them into the *shikara*. Across the canal at Dal Gate was a large, almost new, American sedan. There was a tall stocky man standing beside it wearing a suit and looking a bit over-dressed for Srinagar. Habib was very deferential as he helped him into the *shikara*. 'Habib never puts those cushions in the boat for me and I'm a Princess', said Zina as we watched the *shikara* approach Soul Kiss.

'My name is Shaw, your Highness. I am at your service.' The gentleman introduced himself as Habib hurried to the back to bring out tea.

'What kind of name is Shaw?' asked Zina. 'You don't look English.'

'Actually I'm Persian your Highness, my name is really Shah, but I like Shaw. It has, how do you say it? It has a "ring" to it.'

Habib came back with the tea. As we had tea, Mr Shaw explained to Zina that he knew about the large transfer of dollars her

26

grandmother had sent her to buy Russian sables with. Zina had every money-changer in Srinagar in a tizzy over changing the money, and had been trying to hold one of them to a low number that he had promised her before the money had arrived.

'You see, your Highness, all the money that gets changed in the Vale is changed by me and no one will be able to give you a better price that I am prepared to offer you right now. I must apologise for any misunderstandings you have experienced, I'm sure all the people you have spoken with before me acted in good faith. I am told by Mr Tula that you want to visit Lasa Baba. You will honour me if you and your friends use my car. I'm sure you will find it most comfortable and of course I will arrange for someone to drive you.'

Mr Shaw's car turned out to be perfect. We drove through the foothills that were carpeted with saffron and almonds in blossom. That day turned out to be the culmination of the our time in Srinagar. It was as if we were in a dream. We sat on a gentle hillside overlooking the Vale washed in the pastels of spring blossoms. Lasa Baba sat surrounded by the small group of men that were his disciples. All morning the devotees arrived. Some came with gifts, some brought the sick seeking a miracle, all carried food for the feast. A long trench was dug to make a cooking fire. An area for the sick was cleared with a corner for the mentally disturbed. An hysterical young woman was dragged in front of Lasa Baba. In soft tones he told them to let her go. As he spoke to her she began to relax. He laid his hands on her head and blessed her. All day the women prepared the feast; Lasa Baba gave audiences and ministered to the sick. We sat and watched as he and his disciples rose and began to walk toward a large tree covered in pink blossoms. As they approached the tree all the blossoms fell making a carpet on the ground for them to sit on.

'It's a miracle,' Zina whispered.

'It must have been the wind,' I said.

'I didn't feel any wind baby,' Sacha observed.

Spring was melting the snows on the passes that lead into and out of the Vale of Kashmir. Sacha and Ron left for Dehli and Peter a few days later. I stayed on for a bit longer to help Zina get ready to move. She would not return to the States. She made me promise to visit her mother and grandmother in New York to tell them she was well. I was planning to go home after visiting Tokyo to study the Nōh and Kabuki Theatres.

Bit by bit drugs would cease to be a source of liberation for me and I would live for another twenty-five years in and out of a nightmare before I was finally able to get sober.

A Slow Boat to Tokyo

She [Yoko Ono] invited me to be a part of the performance. I didn't have any idea about what this whole thing was. What was performance? I didn't know. And really there wasn't very much performance art anyway. It was in the very early days of performance art. So I joined in that performance. Tony and I did a performance together. It may have even been Tony's piece. In which we were bound tied together back to back with all kinds of ropes and bottles were tied to the ropes and hanging and dragging on the floor. And the idea was that Tony and I had to walk bound tightly back to back from one side of the stage to the other and back again while Yoko said to the audience 'I just let two snakes loose in the auditorium and you can light one match only to see these two snakes, they might be anywhere in the audience now.' I was terrified; I remember I was sweating profusely . . . Sam Francis was there . . . Jasper Johns was there . . . I found out later, that she was hired as a translator by Merce Cunningham Dance Company. And Peggy Guggenheim was travelling with the company at the time. And so Yoko was hired as the translator. And I think it's in one of the biographies of Peggy Guggenheim where she says she and Yoko were sharing a hotel room.

JEFF PERKINS

SS *Laos*, May 1, 1964

'You've got to meet Yoko Ono. She's extremely hip and a great conceptual artist,' said Jed Curtis.

It was spring and after the winter in India I was on my way to Tokyo. Jed Curtis and I were sitting on the fantail of the freighter *Laos*, moving down the Dong Nai River to the South China Sea

29

from Saigon. Tall rushes and marshes border the Dong Nai. Jed and I had met a week and a half earlier in Colombo. As I was watching people boarding the ship, I saw Jed, this red-bearded bespectacled giant with a sitar and knapsack negotiating the gangway. As it turns out, we were berthed together way down in the bowels of the ship with some Chinese workers and two German students.

The SS *Laos* was working her way to Kobe from Bombay. It was early in the morning on another vivid Southeast Asia day and already hot and humid. To escape the oppressive mugginess below decks, the other passengers, mostly Chinese, were relaxing in the morning sun. I was playing chess with Michael, a gaunt English-man and Buddhist monk, who was travelling to Hong Kong to pick up an inheritance so he could buy an ocean-going junk and sail off into the South Seas.

Jed, who was a concert pianist and composer who had performed with Yoko Ono in New York, was going on about her and playing his sitar. 'I helped her with some of her conceptual events in New York. She's a conceptual composer. She worked with John Cage. She calls her work *Music of the Mind*.'

'Like the happenings that Bob Rauschenberg and Allen Kaprow are doing?' I mused as I pondered a knight fork.

'No, conceptual events are different. They're more planned. They're complete works of art in themselves. I saw her do a series of events at her loft on Chambers Street. After I got to know her, she invited me to take part in a piece she did at The Living Theatre on Fourteenth Street. She goes all the way, she's totally committed to her art.'

'That's so cool, man.' I thought better of the knight fork.

'She was also one of the founders of the Fluxus group. She's a real artistic pioneer,' Jed continued.

CRUMP! Something exploded in the rushes off to starboard. We heard a whistling sound and then there was a god-awful explosion in the water right next to our ship. The passengers ran for cover. I was about to dive under the table when I noticed Michael hadn't stopped studying the chessboard. I decided to sit it out, too. A second mortar went off and we could see the flash in the reeds. As the shell landed even closer to us, the gun ship that was escorting us had the range on the mortar's position and began to pound the Viet Cong.

Michael advanced his knight to avoid the fork.

A week later, Shibuya district Tokyo
'Shush, don't wake the baby. Hi Dan, I'm Tony.'

It was a week later. Jed and I were in the Shibuya district of Tokyo at Yoko Ono and Tony Cox's apartment. Tony Cox was Yoko Ono's husband. Thin, medium height with glasses, he had an air of whimsy about him, mixed with a bit of mischievousness. 'Yoko will be right out. She's just putting Kyoko to sleep.' He slid through the opening in the doorway to meet Jed and me in the dim hallway, and left the door slightly ajar. Tony had a quizzical look on his face as though he was up to something. We began to talk in low voices about art, Zen, and dope.

Through the crack in the door, in the half-light of the tiny apartment, I could see Yoko Ono, a *shibui* face from a Japanese print floating on a pillow with long black hair falling on either side. Her daughter Kyoko, only a few months old, was falling asleep beside her. The apartment was so small. Everything in Tokyo seemed small.

'Dan's a madman. I met him on the boat from Bombay. He goes to the Nōh theatre all day long and is a Beat Zen master,' Jed said to Tony.

Kyoko having finally gone to sleep, Yoko came out to join us in the hallway. 'Are you really a Zen master?' she said in a low voice with a smile on her face as she sat down beside us.

'Not really, I'm just a poet and mime performer. I've come to Tokyo to study the Nōh and Kabuki theatres. Hi, I'm Dan.'

'I'm Yoko. It's always nice to meet another artist.' Her face reminded me of a mask worn by a weeping ghost in a play I had seen that week at the Nōh theatre. She had a coolness and intelligence about her. When she spoke, a smile almost crossed her face.

'Why do you go to the Nōh theatre?' she asked.

'Well, I'm on a leave of absence from the American Mime Theatre in New York. I'm the lead performer and assistant director there and I also teach at the American Academy of Dramatic Arts and the Gene Frankel Theatre Workshop. I love the performing and teaching, but I want more. I've been going to theatres around the world to see how they incorporate mimetic forms. I study their rehearsal process and then see the performance.'

'The world is changing so fast and artists have to change with it. We have to lead with our creativity and our ideas,' Yoko said.

As we talked in hushed voices, sitting on the floor of Tony and Yoko's hallway, I felt that I was making a friend.

I moved in to a small apartment with Jed and we met with Yoko and Tony in the evenings at their apartment or in little restaurants to discuss our work and ideas. During the day, I was continuing my study of the Nōh and Kabuki theatres.

Jed and I were having dinner with Yoko, Tony, and their friend Jeff Perkins, who was helping Yoko with her work. We were sitting in what I thought was the smallest restaurant in the world. We were crowded into a tiny room in the back, sitting around a little table on tatami mats.

'How have you gotten access to the Nōh and Kabuki?' Yoko asked.

'The American National Theatre Academy in Washington gave me papers and a letter introducing me as an American performer and director. The people at the theatres are great – when I showed them the letter, they gave me tickets so I can go to shows whenever I want. The people at the Kanze Kaikan, the

Nōh theatre, have really embraced me. They're letting me come to all their rehearsals and today they asked me to show them some American mime.'

'That must have been intimidating,' said Tony.

'Yeah, I was really nervous, but I just took off my shoes and got up on their beautiful clean white-cypress stage. I stood very still and tried to control myself. Then I let my body fill with energy and began to move in a slow and stately manner. I did a variation on one of their characters, a god who descends onto the stage from heaven. They loved it. Then I showed them how I could make the character transform into other characters using only my body.'

'It's really great that you can communicate without words,' said Yoko, taking a bit of food.

The conversation turned to her plans. She was putting together some of her conceptual pieces for a major show at the Sogetsu Art Center. As we were leaving, we found out that the little room we were eating in was the private space of the family who owned the restaurant. They were too polite to say anything.

'Tony is a better calligrapher than me. Get him to put the Japanese characters on your sign,' said Yoko, sitting on the bed that seems to be the only furniture in their apartment. We had become good friends. She was translating one of my poems, and I was going to put it on a sign to help my street performance. Out of hash, out of money, I had taken to performing on the street. The poem described me as a fish swimming in the ocean of the world. I would write a poem in water on the street, draw a picture, or do a little mime bit for money. I was at it for three days and had raised about $100. I needed a sign in Japanese, so Yoko was translating my poem and Tony was putting it on a piece of canvas with a brush and black ink. I had painted the fish on it and had a bamboo pole to hang it on.

Over the previous weeks, I had learned a lot about Yoko. I was surprised to learn that this avant-garde artist living in this tiny apartment was from a very prominent Tokyo family. Her mother came from one of the richest banking families in Japan, and her father, who gave up a career as a concert pianist, was a banker. When she was a little girl, she went to Gakashuin, the most prestigious private school in Japan, where some her classmates were children of the Emperor. She studied the piano from an early age then received instruction in opera. In 1952, Yoko's father was transferred to New York and her family moved to Scarsdale. She studied music at Sarah Lawrence College and then became involved in the avant-garde music scene and moved downtown. Her parents were very upset and pretty much disowned her. She did various things to get by, like teaching music in the public schools and being a janitor in order to get a free loft space to live in.

During this period, her loft on Chambers Street became one of the centres of the growing avant-garde art scene. Working with people like John Cage and minimalist composer La Monte Young, she began to stage Zen-like events that involved the audience and went beyond what was done in music to date. With George Macuias and other artistic pioneers, she was one of the founders of the Fluxus movement.

Yoko was in Tokyo for over a year. Tony, a big fan of hers, had come over from New York to see her and they ended up getting married. She had been very busy, putting together her conceptual pieces for a show at the Sogetsu Art Center. I was going back to the States before the show, so I planned to get together with her in New York to see one of her performances.

The sign worked great. People read it and lined up to meet me, get a poem, a picture, an autograph, or just to shake my hand. I put the money in a plastic bag. In just a few hours I had enough for a flight to Vancouver and the train across Canada to home. The crowd attracted the police.

'You can't do that on the street, it's illegal,' the police officers told me, but they were quite curious and ended up escorting me to the American Express office so that I could buy my air ticket.

I went to Yoko's to thank her for translating my poem and tell her and Tony about my success. Before I left we planned to meet again in New York.

You Can't Go Home Again

I returned to the States after Tokyo and spent the summer at my parents' house in Provincetown on Cape Cod. I had changed so much during my year away and everything seemed very constricted. I wasn't ready to go back to the Mime Theatre and my old life of performing and teaching in New York. I was smoking pot all the time now and I felt this deep need to be free to live on impulse without schedules and obligations. I painted and wrote poetry in a little room with its own entrance off the cellar of our family house on Cook street a few feet from the sun-washed bay dotted with fishing boats. With the Provincetown sand in my shoes and a year of new experiences and dreams roiling in my head, I was exploding with creativity. Paintings and collages began to fill the little room and each night small groups of us would sit and smoke grass as we talked about the hip scene and read our writing to each other.

I gave a few very successful mime lecture demonstrations, but my heart was not in it. Something had happened to me and I just couldn't return to my old life. I was more interested in having visions that performing. Zina wrote to me from Athens describing the small but very hip scene there. She was almost ready to give up the world and wanted to have a bit of a fling before she became a Tibetan nun. Ronnie Vial was with her.

My father had shown my paintings to the artist Peter Busa who insisted I meet Walter Chrysler, the heir to the motor company. Walter collected paintings and painters and really liked my work. He bought some of my paintings and hung them in his museum, a large old Methodist Church he had converted into a gallery in which to exhibit his extensive collection. He encouraged me to paint large canvasses and introduced me to people who could help my career.

'I want you to come to New York this Fall Dan, I'll set you up in a studio; I think you have a wonderful career ahead of you.' Walter and I were sitting on a bench in front of his museum watching the colourful summer Provincetown crowd walk by with the sunlit bay beyond.

'I don't know Walter – I'm not ready to go back to New York.'

'Well I hope you'll think about it Dan. I can help you get started on a very successful career. You're a good artist and with my support and connections, I'm sure you'll go a long way.'

'I promise to consider it very seriously Walter; I'll get back to you in a few days.' I knew I wasn't going to take him up on it. I didn't want to paint for money and I suspected he wanted to fuck me. I saw the whole art world as phony and unreal. I couldn't wait to get to Athens and see Zina and Ronnie. From there I would go back to India. I was going to get away from this uptight world driven by power, money, and sex.

Was I turning my back on becoming a successful artist because the addiction was already beginning to distort my thinking? Was it really because I valued my freedom so much? The whole straight life style was hypocritical, shallow, and phony. I was going to live my life free, unencumbered, and without regrets. Besides, the States was a lousy place to get busted.

I left Provincetown with Johnny Mills. I met Johnny in Provincetown that summer and we had become good friends. He was a lanky skinny kid from Jersey who always seemed to have the best grass and was always ready to do the next hip thing. He was fascinated by my stories of India and wanted to leave the States. He and I joined Zina and Ronnie in Athens. Ron, Johnny and I found a place to rent at number 2, Dafnomili, high up on Lykavittos hill. The old house sat baking in the sun with a view over Athens, Piraeus, and the sea beyond. We were joined by an array of hip characters; Johnny's friend Psychedelic Ben, Peter 'Skyfuck' Zimmels, Ron Zimardi and many more. Out on the island of Hydra, the beautiful Marianne was living with her boyfriend, the Canadian poet Leonard Cohen, who wanted to turn his poems into songs. I met my first wife, Jill, a young English woman who had left her studies in French poetry at the Sorbonne to live the beat life in Morocco. She had landed in Athens with stories of the underground scene in Morocco where she had worked on the poetry review *Gnaoua* with Ira Cohen. Together Jill and I published a poetry review called *Residu* that embodied the new hip ethos that had taken over my life.

Across the sun-bleached roofs below our window I could see the Acropolis with the Parthenon in the middle distance. Two and a half thousand years of European history stretched out before me. According to Aristotle, Athenian tragedy had arisen during the fifth century BC at the ritual of the Dionysian dithyramb. Each spring, at the tragedies, actors would compete to be possessed by the God. The audiences, experiencing and identifying with the sufferings of the protagonists, would be possessed as well. Sitting in my house in Athens I thought that at last mankind was shedding the dark cloak that had slowly covered us since then and kept us from a direct connection with the Gods. Through the sacraments of consciousness expansion we were re-establishing our natural connection to the Gods. *Residu* was to be incomplete. The poetry and drawings in it were just shadows or artifacts left from the greater experiences we were having that could only be lived and never shared completely.

In Athens I had my first real encounter with heroin. I have always had the strength and the weakness of going all the way and I wanted to experience all that drugs had to offer. Being a sober addict and alcoholic now since 1985, I know that all addicts think the same thing – 'I can control it.' Back then I really believed that I would not be consumed by the flames of drug addiction. I thought I had joined a new brotherhood, explorers in consciousness expansion. We were travelling to a new land where the fruits of our journey would so outweigh the costs that I would be able to stop using heroin with at worst a few uncomfortable days. I had erroneously concluded that the dire tales one heard about drug use was a mixture of propaganda from the liquor industry, the prejudices of square culture, and problems that were really caused by the social oppression of black people. Looking back now from the perspective of twenty-three years of sobriety, I see a fragile moth fluttering rapidly toward the flame of addiction, completely ignorant of how it entrenches itself. I had never even heard the word 'denial' used as a symptom of this disease I didn't know I had.

I received letters from someone in London addressed to 'Dr Benway c/o Dan Richter'.[1] They contained small amounts of pharmaceutical heroin. During the late nights spent working on the manuscripts, high above the lights of Athens and high on hashish and heroin, Jill and I fell in love.

I think that's when I first recognised the Beatles. I must have heard them the summer before in the States. Their music was being played everywhere, but I don't remember hearing it. In Athens, we listened to the radio late at night as we worked preparing *Residu* for the printers. In the early hours, the radio picked up a lot more stations and we often searched for Radio Cairo and the incredible Egyptian singer, Oum Kalthoum. One night I came across 'The Beatles', happy upbeat voices. But the song we were all obsessed by at that time was Martha and the Vandellas' *Dancing in the Streets*. We played it at full volume and danced round the house. It symbolised the change in the air, new energy and freedom – with kids all over the world coming as they were to dance in the streets.

1   Dr Benway is a character in William Burroughs's *The Naked Lunch*.

I let a room on the ground floor to Johnny's friend, Psychedelic Ben. Ben Goldstein, intelligent with a quirky sense of humour, was into psychedelics in a very big way. He set himself up as a drug company and placed an order for a very large amount of mescaline which arrived for him at Dafnomili. We spent an afternoon searching for a large apothecary's scale. We finally found one in a wooden cabinet, protected by glass panels. My vision of a life of constantly expanding consciousness was becoming a reality.

In London Hip is Becoming Cool

In the spring of 1965 our poetry review *Residu* was completed. We had gathered hip new writing and artwork from great poets and artists in both Europe and the States. We stowed boxes full of *Residus* and with Ben Goldstein in the back seat of a borrowed car, set off enthusiastically for London. In England, I knew there was a program where addicts could register and be given heroin legally. I planned to sell my *Residus* and become a legal addict in order to continue my dangerous experiments with expanded consciousness.

On the tree-lined streets of London, the late spring sun shone through the leaves and dappled everything with light. Flowers bloomed in profusion in window boxes, front gardens and in the numerous parks and squares. The music of the Beatles was everywhere. Arriving from mainland Europe one was aware of an order and cleanliness that was comforting but mildly constricting. London, like an aging empress, still seemed to watch over much of the world with an intimacy and tolerance that appeared to arise from the variety of people who had come from every corner of the globe.

We settled in Notting Hill Gate, just Northwest of Kensington and Chelsea, which was where it was all happening. Everywhere you could see young hip faces. The cheap little flats, known as 'bed-sits', were filling up with long-haired young people with guitars, dreams and pot. Alexander Trocchi[2] had a bed-sit there that Jill and I began to hang out at. Alex was a craggy Scots Beat writer and

2 Alexander Trocchi was born in Glasgow in 1925. In the late fifties Alex wrote *Cain's Book* which created quite a stir as an instant beat classic. By the time of his death in 1984, he had cut a colorful swathe through many of the important cultural movements in both Europe and America. A

junkie with an insatiable appetite for heroin, people, ideas, women, and booze.

'Ronnie, meet Dan Richter, he's a poet and a voyager in the realm of consciousness expansion. Dan say hello to R. D. Laing. He's doing great work with schizophrenics and psychedelics.'

R. D. Laing was a tweedy intellectual and, like Alex, a Scotsman. A radical psychiatrist and author, he had already achieved notoriety with his books and his clinic.

Alex seemed to know everybody on the literary drug scene. Our friendship with him put us right in the centre of what was happening in the drug culture. His place reeked of junk and he knew all about the English programme to register addicts. In Twelve Step Programmes we talked about the insanity of the disease of addiction and alcoholism. In retrospect, that is the only way I can explain the madness of my behaviour at that time. I wasn't even physically addicted but I wanted to present myself as an addict. If I could convince a doctor to register me, so I could get prescriptions for free legal heroin. Alex couldn't have been more helpful. He had a Mephistophelian side to him. I was able to arrange an appointment with a famous drug doctor named Lady Frankau.

'This is so cool, Jill. If she takes me on I can have all the heroin and cocaine I want and then when I've finished experimenting I can arrange a controlled detoxification and come down gently. And it will all be legal.'

Jill wasn't so sure, but I was not going to be dissuaded by anyone. I intended to experience being a junkie in a safe and controlled way.

Before my first meeting with Lady Frankau, I put extra needle

---

controversial figure, described variously as a junkie, outsider, literary outlaw, visionary, philosopher, underground organizer and antique book dealer, Alex rubbed shoulders with many of the great names of modern literature. Allen Ginsberg, Samuel Beckett, William Burroughs, Eugene Ionesco, Norman Mailer, Jean Genet, Timothy Leary, R. D. Laing and many others fell into his orbit of influence.

marks in my arm so that I would look convincing. Alex had been supplying me with heroin, but I really wasn't addicted yet.

'Yes ma'm, I've been using for a while now and I want to be legal.'

Across a little Edwardian desk sat Lady Frankau, an aristocratic lady in tweed suits with a gold lorgnette hanging round her neck on a black velvet ribbon. 'How much heroin are you using?'

'Well ma'm, about five or six grains of heroin and about the same amount of cocaine', I lied.

She raised the lorgnette and took a closer look at me.

'I'll start you out on half of that. If you feel sick, call me and I can adjust the dose.'

Lady Frankau, who specialised in treating heroin addicts, had her office at 32 Wimpole Street. After you rang the doorbell, Mrs Clarke, her companion, would usher you into a wood-panelled waiting room with expensive oriental carpets on the floor. The room looked like it had been designed by Sir Arthur Conan Doyle. When Lady Frankau was ready for you, Mrs Clarke led you into a tiny, wood-panelled elevator that took you up to a little office, all dark wood, leather, and velvet. It looked more like a very small Edwardian study than a doctor's office.

Lady Frankau was convinced that addicts needed to be stabilised. With a constant and controlled supply of heroin and cocaine, they would not go through the up-and-down cycle of withdrawal followed by getting high again. She believed that by stabilising addicts she could calm them down enough to consider detoxification. Jill and I loved her. She was quite a character. If one of her addicts was having a problem with the authorities, she would pick up her phone and call someone high up in the government. The matter would usually be resolved in short order. It was rumoured that she counted among her patients addicts and alcoholics in very high places. One suspected she might even be able to get the Queen or the Prime Minister on the phone to straighten out a particularly knotty situation.

As time went by and my foolish experiment turned into a nightmare, she became my refuge in a storm. She made me feel safe and took away the fear addicts have of not being able to get that next all-important fix.

I'm constantly asked why I used heroin. After twenty-six years of sobriety, it's pretty clear – I was an addict. I know the so-called reasons I had when I started: 'OK, I'm going to be like Huxley and Burroughs, I'm going to expand my consciousness and see the face of God.' People would say, 'If you take enough speed and stay up for five days, you'll see God.' It's a symptom of addiction, that heroic justification, always finding some noble reason for getting high. Addicts trick themselves, that's why in sobriety you constantly have to watch out for your own mind. You will tell yourself that there is a perfectly good reason for using, but it's the disease trying to trick you.

During the period in London when I was becoming progressively more addicted, I was justifying it. I was excited about what I was doing. I would tell myself I was becoming a voyager in inner space, it would make me a better artist. But in reality I was locked in the iron grip of an addiction. I was just an addict and I paid the price.

'It's Allen Ginsberg and he's fucking naked.' The Liverpool accent was unmistakable; it was John Lennon.

I was standing with Jill at a major bash in London for our friend, the Beat poet Allen Ginsberg. It was June 3, 1965 and we were celebrating Allen's thirty-ninth birthday. He was standing in a corner, stark naked with a drink in his hand, surrounded by people trying to get a peep at him. He loved to take his clothes off, especially in a crowd. I turned to see John standing with the other Beatles. They were staring at Allen with amused looks on their faces. The Beat scene was spreading into the mainstream. In London, being hip was becoming cool.

A couple of weeks before, I had met Allen for the first time. I was sitting in Alex Trocchi's flat when Allen arrived. He was wearing a cotton suit jacket with a blue button-down shirt and a preppy rep tie. He had long hair and a beard, blue jeans, and sneakers, but I was taken aback by the tie. The fire in his eyes that I could see through his plastic-rimmed glasses confirmed his hipness. A crowd of us was there to welcome him to London's hip literary scene. Allen regaled us with accounts of his recent experiences in Eastern Europe. He was elected 'King of the May' by thousands of students during the May Day celebrations in Prague. They were carrying him through the streets in a chair, preparing to crown him, when the Czech authorities intervened. They called him an 'immoral menace' and expelled him from the country. He narrowly escaped arrest on drug charges.

'I'm going to be on the evening news here in London tomorrow night,' Allen went on. 'It's really incredible how much publicity they're giving me.'

We all decided that if we planned a poetry reading, Allen could mention it on the news and lots of people would come.

'How about that?' It was the next day, and Jill and I were searching for a place to hold the reading.

'How about what, Dan?'

'That, over there. The Albert Hall,' I said.

'Don't be daft, Dan, they don't have poetry readings there.'

We had been looking all over London at small venues and had found nothing. Tired, we walked into Hyde Park to smoke a joint and were sitting on the steps of the Albert Memorial, on the south side of the park across from the Albert Hall. The Royal Albert Hall is an immense, oval Victorian hall that Queen Victoria erected in honour of her late husband, Prince Albert. It seats close to five thousand people and is used as a venue for concerts, boxing matches, and events that need to accommodate large groups of people.

'Actually, think about it, Jill, Allen is a passionate salesman and people are going to want to come, even if just out of curiosity. I have a feeling this just might work.'

We stood up and crossed the road. A side door took us up a flight of wide Victorian stairs into the booking office.

'We have a cancellation the night of June 11th. You could have the hall then, sir. It would be £800 for the evening,' said a little man in a tweed jacket and tie sitting behind a large hardwood desk.

We had just decided to get married and Jill had a £500 cheque her father had given her from an insurance policy. We excused ourselves and went over to a corner of the room, where we whispered to each other for a few moments. Jill thought I was crazy but finally agreed. Turning to the man in the tweed jacket, I said, 'Would you take a deposit of £500?'

Somehow we did it; on June 11, 1965 we held a gigantic poetry reading at the Royal Albert Hall. We called it *Wholly Communion.* Allen went on TV and told everyone to come and, to our astonishment, we sold out. At least seven to eight thousand people showed up and we had to turn many of them away. We had organised the event in a series of chaotic meetings mainly at Alex Trocchi's place. Poets convened from all over Europe. Beat poets Gregory Corso and Lawrence Ferlinghetti came over from Paris, the Russian poet Andrei Voznesensky was in the audience, and we had a tape of William Burroughs reading from some of his latest work.

'Change is in the air, Danny.' My friend, New Zealand producer and poet John Esam, and I were talking excitedly backstage waiting to go on. 'Bob Dylan, the Beatles, the whole world is waking up to a hipper universe,' he continued.

'What happened?' I asked, amazed at the thousands of turned-on young people who were filling the hall.

'I don't know, but let's enjoy it,' said John, as we walked onto the stage with five thousand people watching us.

A Telegram to Chairman Mao

In 1965 a bunch of weird beards gathered at the Park Hotel, Cardiff. Most of them weren't even wearing ties. A poetry conference was taking place in the city as part of the Commonwealth Arts Festival. Amongst the stellar line-up of bards were writer Alexander Trocchi, Michael X, George Macbeth, Adrian Henri, Mike Horovitz, Dan Richter, Brian Patten and future Nobel Prize winner Wole Soyinka.

Anthony Brockway http://babylonwales.blogspot.com

Poetry had become heroic again. Even before Rock and Roll had broken free, poetry had liberated itself and become a vehicle for change. Allen Ginsberg, Gregory Corso, Lawrence Ferlinghetti and the other poets spoke their poetry; they didn't just write it. From the beginning the Beats carried a message of change and liberation. They didn't want to be accepted by the establishment, they wanted it to change as they called into question every aspect of a stilted, uptight society.

By the early sixties the young people were listening to the Beats and their Jazz and folk music. The Albert Hall reading was full of passion and a desire for change. The rallying cries were to end the Vietnam War, ban the bomb, get high and get hip to what was happening.

Riding on the energy that came out of the Albert Hall reading, a group of us led by Alex Trocchi were invited to be delegates to the first Commonwealth Poetry Conference. It was part of the Commonwealth Festival in Cardiff. Alex, his usual rugged self with his chin pushed forward, looking like he had just come out of a bar fight, led the group onto the train from London. We were a motley crew with our beards and shades. I was wearing black bell-bottoms bought in Amsterdam and a short leather jacket. Jill looked lovely as usual in a big white hat and a flowered pants suit from a hip little shop called Biba. When we arrived in Cardiff we immediately created a ruckus. The Commonwealth Festival was a pretty run-of-the-mill, British event. We arrived riding on the energy from the success of Albert Hall, aware that thousands of people were listening to us. This was the first inkling of this big explosion that was taking place and we were right in the front of it. Michael X, head of the British Black Muslims, proposed sending a telegram to Chairman Mao suggesting he should use palms as weapons instead of bombs. Everyone was arguing about how to word it. The Vietnam War was a topic on everyone's mind. Alex decided to do a demonstration with a Vietnamese pig, but the stodgy Conference organisers drew the line at the idea of having a pig on stage.

In the balcony at the back of the auditorium, the poet, Harry Fainlight sat silently like a falcon on a perch observing everybody. He had a bow and arrow in his hands. He had pierced the conference catalogue with the arrow as a form of protest. On the last night of the conference someone took all the shoes left in front of peoples' hotel doors for the porters to shine and threw them down an elevator shaft.

The conference was a rowdy, exciting experience indicative of the times. The energy and excitement were palpable and the changes were happening so quickly. We felt like we were flying at the speed of sound with the wind blowing our hair back and rumpling our clothes as we catapulted into this new future, this new society, this new world. Martin Luther King was inspiring black people in the US and the blacks in Africa were moving towards independence. We felt that we too had the power to stop this foolish war and to start people thinking differently and living differently. It was exciting and exhilarating.

It was at the conference that I met Michael X for the first time, observed him in action and noticed the light in his eyes. Afterwards, I saw him several times at Alex's. He would stop by and read us the love poems he had written to his girlfriend, Nancy Bacal. She was a lovely, intelligent woman with a wonderful smile and curly red hair. Michael was very much in love with her. I published two of the poems in the second issue of *Residu*. I learned that Michael had been an enforcer, a hood, for Peter Rachman, a slumlord in the fifties in the Notting Hill area. Many of us lived in this part of London which had evolved into a fashionable area, near the Portobello Market. Michael used to be a thug collecting rents from poor people but somewhere along the line, he met Malcolm X. Malcolm told him, 'Michael, you've got all these leadership skills and this personal power and you're using it against your people. You're one of the oppressors. Why don't you turn around and use it to help liberate them.' Michael was touched by this and changed his name from Michael de Freitas to Michael X. He became the leader of the Black Muslims in England. He came from Trinidad and his father had been a Portuguese trader. Like many colonials, he had come to London and fought his way up through the ghetto. He was a very impressive man, stocky with a mass of curly hair. He had passionate eyes that looked right at you and a wonderful smile. When he spoke, whatever he said seemed very important and you knew he would back it up.

'If we can control the source of LSD we can control the world.' Tim Leary, Psychedelic Ben, and I had been sitting all afternoon in a Forte's café in Knightsbridge eating French fries and deciding the fate of the world. Riding the wave of change that had brought us all to London, Tim was going on about how acid would liberate and change the world.

'Why would we want to control the world?' I said, as I took another mouthful of fries and ketchup. 'Let's just set it free.'

During this period, heroin was fast becoming more than an

experiment in consciousness expansion. In a very short time, I was not able to stop. I guess I never believed that I would become addicted. I certainly had no idea what addiction meant. Until you feel the sickness that withdrawal brings there is no way to fathom how terrible it is. The physical side is bad enough, but the psychological is devastating.

One of the upshots of the Albert Hall and the Commonwealth Poetry Conference was that I was gaining a degree of notoriety. When Jill and I got married our picture appeared on the front page of the *Evening Standard* under the caption, 'Artist Jill marries poet Dan' and there was an interview with us with another picture of us sitting in our little bed-sit with me reading a poem. The BBC picked up on this since the public was really interested in hippy beatnik people and the whole drug counter culture.

I was invited a number of times to go on BBC talk shows. I can remember one bizarre interview on LSD where there were shots of me on a roof with the skyline of London in the background. I had my little round circular shades on and a cow skull in my lap. I guess I had just picked up the skull for effect. I remember Alex Trocchi saying to me, 'Dan, take this cow skull and keep it with you. It will be great.'

This notoriety soon brought problems.

Late one night Jill and I were woken by a pounding on the door. Voices were shouting,

'Police! Police! Open the door! Open the door!'

I had a lump of hash beside the bed. I immediately picked it up and ran over to the little kitchen area, where I shoved it into a box of corn flakes. Meanwhile Jill slowly opened the door. Three cops came barrelling in and started shouting, 'We know you have drugs here.'

I moved between them and Jill, and tried to talk to them.

'Listen, I'm a legal addict,' I said.

But that didn't satisfy them. They already knew I was a registered addict. They were looking for LSD, marijuana, anything illegal. I had made the mistake of discussing LSD on television. They knew if they found these substances they could bust me. The situation deteriorated when they began shoving me against the wall. There was one goon in a blue-grey, phony sharkskin suit and a sleazy silk tie. I remember staring at his tie pin with a picture of a Thai dancer. Really ugly! I kept thinking 'now I am going to get beaten up.' I was watching his hands as they began to clench. At that point, Jill broke loose from the other two, ran out into the hallway and started yelling to wake the other tenants. She kept shouting, 'The police are here and they're beating up my husband! The police are here and they're beating up my husband! The police are here and they're beating up my husband!'

Doors opened, people came out in the hall and the police seemed to decide this wasn't good for their image. The guy with the Thai dancer on his tie clip let me go and the three of them left with some parting threats.

I immediately closed the door, and called Alex Trocchi. He had been with me on the television programme and I guessed he would also receive a visit. Luckily I was able to warn him ten minutes before the police arrived. He was able to clean up his flat and keep out of jail that night.

'Over my dead body.' A stocky nun with a male saint's name was standing at the top of the stairs that led to the garden below. I was taking a cure in Bethany Nursing Home in North London.

'Sister I have to leave. I'm going to leave.' For three days I had been lying in a private room alternating between chills and sweats, nauseous, miserable, and delirious as the heroin left my body. My doctor, Lady Frankau, had sent me there.

I remember feeling like a trapped animal. As the cure progressed the brutal, merciless onslaught of the withdrawal sickness overwhelmed me. Outside the window there was a garden and at the bottom, a ten foot wall. Against the wall stood a statue of Jesus with his arms outstretched. As I lay in my bed I began to form a plan. I would sneak out at night and climb up on to Jesus and from there I could reach the top of the wall and freedom.

'I'm leaving sister – please get out of my way,' my voice was shaking.

I pushed past her, knocking her against the wall, and ran down the stairs. I rushed out into the garden with the flustered sister chasing me. It was dark but I could make out the silhouette of the statue. In a few seconds I was up on his shoulders and over the wall. As I landed on the other side I saw a taxi approaching. I hailed it.

'Where to, Guv?' the driver asked as he eyed my rumpled appearance.

'4 Observatory Gardens, it's in Kensington, just off Church Street.'

I had snuck a call to Alex Trocchi from Bethany. Alex always had dope. I would be high and 'well' in half an hour.

Our magazine *Residu,* which we had brought to London from Greece, was full of the latest underground poetry including two poems by Ginsberg that had never been published before. Looking for some one to sell it in London, we struck up a friendship with Barry Miles and his wife Sue. Miles sold *Residu* for us. He was the owner of Indica Books. He had started out at Better Books in Charing Cross Road, and had made Indica *the* hip bookshop – an underground clearing house for books, reviews, pamphlets, and people. Miles, skinny, erudite, and bespectacled, with an unruly shock of dirty blond hair, was the purveyor of everything hip in literature.

Miles, Peter Asher, and John Dunbar had formed a company called MAD Co. It was short for Miles, Asher, and Dunbar. They set up Indica Books and Gallery in Mason's Yard in Mayfair. Miles ran the new bookshop and John, the gallery. Just as Miles had the corner on all that was new and hip in literature in London,

John's Indica Gallery had exhibitions of the latest work from the burgeoning underground art scene.

The Beatles were seen everywhere in London. Paul McCartney was the first one of them I met. Paul was involved with MAD Co. through his friendship with Miles.

With the gigantic success of the Albert Hall reading and *Residu* on sale at Indica, Jill and I found ourselves in the middle of the hip scene with lots of poetry readings and passionate meetings to discuss what was happening in London and the rest of the world.

We made a lot of new friends. Among them were John Dunbar and his new wife, the young singing star Marianne Faithful. Marianne was very pregnant and Jill had just become so to. We were bright young couples both with children on the way.

Marianne was very young and beautiful with an aura of vulner-ability and innocence. Just a few years out of convent school she had begun her career playing guitar and singing folk ballads. The Rolling Stones manager, Andrew Oldham, was impressed by her singing and fragile little girl looks. He encouraged Mick Jagger and Keith Richards to write *As Tears Go By* for her. The recording was released in 1964 and she was catapulted into stardom.

Marianne and John invited us over for dinner a few weeks after their son Nicholas was born. They lived in a top floor flat in Lennox Gardens in Chelsea. John showed us into a big L-shaped room, which had a large sofa, some chairs, and a dining table. There were three windows looking out on the leafy trees of the gardens below.

'Can I get you a drink?' John asked. 'Marianne is cooking and Nicholas's nanny is putting him to bed.'

As John poured our drinks, we could hear Marianne in the kitchen. We went and stuck our heads in to say Hi.

'This is the first time I've cooked duck and it seems to be coming out OK. I do hope you like it,' she said with both excitement and trepidation. 'I'm also cooking these little French peas.'

Tiny the nanny, who was more like a giant, came down the hall from Nicholas's room to tell Marianne that he was asleep and she was going home.

The ducks turned out well and we had a lovely dinner. As we were finishing, there was a knock on the door.

When John opened it, there stood Paul McCartney carrying a very big hobbyhorse.

'Hi, look what I found for Nicholas,' he said.

Paul was just back from a Beatles tour in America. After introductions, we all admired the hobbyhorse. It was very large.

'It'll be a while before Nicholas can use it,' said John, and we all laughed.

Paul pulled an envelope of marijuana out of his pocket and explained that Bob Dylan had given it to him. He also said that Bob had introduced the Beatles to pot for the first time last August in New York when they were staying at the Hotel Delmonico on Park Avenue. I found it hard to believe that they were so new to turning on. John was around the Beatles a lot. He was with them at the Adlib Club awhile before and, when he lit up a pipe of dope, John Lennon was shocked. 'Are they really that square?' I thought.

'I don't know how to roll it,' Paul said.

We all laughed as that was not a problem for us.

Paul put the envelope on the coffee table. We settled down in the big comfortable sofa and I pulled out a packet of Bambu rolling papers and rolled a joint. It was pretty good grass with a definite Mexican flavour to it. As the joint circulated, everyone began to loosen up. Soon talk turned to play and we started laughing and making up silly songs.

Somehow we all ended up sitting on a rug in the center of John and Marianne's living room. To accompany our singing, we brought pots and pans in from the kitchen to use as instruments.

When it came time to leave, Paul offered to drive Jill and I home to Notting Hill Gate in his little Mini Cooper S.

David

I thought I had achieved success. My new lifestyle had meant giving up the familiar world of the brilliant young mime in New York and throwing myself into a new existence, believing I would land on my feet. I was reading my poetry in large gatherings and it was being published. Aside from my writing I was drawing and painting and having settled in London I was beginning to perform again as a mime. I was teaching private mime and movement classes for professionals, eager to put the ideas about movement that I had developed since leaving New York into practice. I had become a minor celebrity since the Albert Hall reading and we were travelling in the hip literary circles and making regular appearances on BBC talk shows.

At the start of 1966 Jill had become pregnant and we were attempting to live a much healthier lifestyle. Lady Frankau had sent me back to Bethany to get clean. Rehab was even more brutal this time. The sister was very understanding and they kept me sedated as I went through the detox. Ten days later, weak and pale, Jill put me in a cab and brought me home. Cleaned up, career taking off, and with a new baby on the way our future looked great.

David was a beautiful baby. He was the answer to all our prayers. He represented our new life that was going to be free of hard drugs. The three of us moved into a little mews house off the Portobello road right in the section that on Saturdays became part of the Portobello Market.

Denbigh Close is one of those charming little London Mews. The uneven cobbled pavement and the tiny buildings that were once stables had been turned into fashionable *pied-à-terres*. Number four belonged to our friend Michael Taylor, a curator at the British Museum. Michael had a relaxed air of casual elegance and insouciance about him. He had a neat reddish brown beard and a posh accent. During the leisurely spring days of Jill's pregnancy we spent a lot of time with Michael and his girl friend Jill listening to Bach and the Beach Boys and talking about literature and Eastern Art. In June, Michael was off for an extended stay in Japan and had asked us to house-sit Denbigh Close for him.

One horrible night in September a horrified Jill shook me awake. I woke to see her holding David's lifeless body; he was not breathing. What followed was a nightmare – hurried CPR as we waited what seemed an interminable time for the ambulance. The cold hospital at night and then the unimaginable talk with the sombre doctor followed by the complete horror of what had happened as we went numbly back to Denbigh Close.

The doctors said it was crib death and that was that – death had taken David from us and we were left shattered and empty. Weeping and ravaged we went home. I was broken and guilty because I was a dry addict. I decided to die. I went to my chemist and lied that a prescription for heroin would be there in the morning from Lady Frankau. In my despair I took the heroin home, cooked up what I thought was a lethal dose and gave myself a shot. I didn't die; I must have had so much adrenalin in my body from the shock of David's death that the heroin wasn't enough. After lying in a coma for a few hours I woke up groggy with a terrible headache. Not only had I lost a son, I was back using heroin.

Over the next months we lived our life like ghosts, empty and terribly alone. In my depression, I was using heroin again with a vengeance. Within a few weeks I was as hooked as I had ever been. Trying to fend off the despair, I threw myself back into teaching mime. It felt good to use my body and inspire other performers.

David's death has never left me. To this day I find myself

thinking about him. How old would he be? What would his voice sound like? What would have he become? For us the emptiness and sorrow was indescribable.

Somehow the time did pass and one morning about a month later the phone rang.

'Danny it's John Esam. A crazy thing happened mate, do you know the American director Stanley Kubrick?'

'Of course I do Johnny, *Paths of Glory, The Killing, Dr Strangelove*, I love his work, what about him?'

'Well, he's making this picture called *2001: A Space Odyssey* and he wants to see you.'

'Don't fuck with me Johnny, I'm not in the mood.'

'No, I'm serious man, he needs a mime and my friend Mike Wilson who works with Arthur C. Clarke mentioned it to me. I said I knew the best mime in London. Mike told Arthur and they want to see you, I'm serious.'

Stanley Kubrick was a rumpled, whimsical, obsessive genius and we liked each other from the first moment we met. He described his dilemma to me. The movie's opening sequence, which featured a tribe of early man-apes from three million years ago, had to be made. He had already shot the live action parts of the picture, but every attempt to shoot the opening sequence hadn't worked and he needed a fresh approach.

'You need to grab the audience right away; you need to create a willing suspension of belief,' I told Stanley excitedly. 'They have to believe these apes are real. It's an acting problem and I'm sure I can solve it. All my training and work has been about how to extend the acting process into movement to create large motivated characters.' Looking back I can't believe how cocky I was. I guess I didn't think he was going to offer me a job. I thought he just wanted to pick a mime's brains to get some new insights into the problem.

'Sounds good Dan, but how do I know you can do it? We've just met and I haven't seen anything you've done.'

'If you give me twenty minutes, a stage, a black leotard, and some towels to stuff in it, I'll show you,' I said, with the enthusiastic hubris of youth.

It worked. I played different characters for Stanley and he loved it. There was Joe the pushy paranoid who got angry when Stanley talked and the scared little neurotic that jumped at the slightest sound. Suddenly Stanley saw real characters instead of a performer in a costume; he could see how it would work. I was hired by him to be his choreographer for the sequence which he and Arthur Clarke called *The Dawn of Man*. All of a sudden, the sad and starving beatnik poet, mime teacher and junkie was transformed into a Hollywood choreographer.[3]

But I had a new problem. Since David's death I had become severely addicted to heroin again and now I had to work round the clock for Stanley. There was no time for rehabs or cures.

3 The book *Moonwatcher's Memoir* covers the period from the fall of 1966 until the beginning of 1968, when Dan worked with Stanley Kubrick on *2001: A Space Odyssey*.

Yoko Ono Comes to Town

Miss Yoko Ono, who came to London on the wave of auto-destructive events which attracted so many Americans, has struck out on her own Zen path towards what she calls 'Concept Art'. After giving several successful and highly professional 'concerts,' she will now appear at Indica Gallery (November 9–22) in a one-lady show of 'Instruction Paintings'.

Art & Artists, November 1966

Number 3 Palace Court – London, December 1966

'Yoko even met a Beatle at the Indica Gallery. John Lennon climbed her ladder piece and then talked to her. I don't think she really knows who the Beatles are.'

It was a few days before Christmas 1966 and I had been working on *2001* for two months. Tony Cox and I were sitting at the kitchen table. Tony was regaling me with reports of Yoko's show that opened the month before at John Dunbar's Indica Gallery. We had run into each other at the gallery and this was the first chance we'd had to catch up.

'John Dunbar is a good friend; he has a great little gallery,' I said as I poured him some tea. The juxtaposition of Yoko and John Lennon seemed so strange. They were from such different worlds – light years apart.

Yoko had come to town for a symposium on destruction in art at the Roundhouse. She was creating quite a stir in the art world with pieces like her *Cut Piece*, where she sat motionless while members of the audience were invited to come on to the stage and cut pieces of her clothing off with a pair of scissors.

Tony was wearing dark-rimmed glasses and had his usual quirky smile. Through the door to the sitting room, I could see that Jill and Yoko, who had just met for the first time, were getting to know each other. Sitting on a Victorian sofa, they were bathed in cool December light. Kyoko, Yoko and Tony's daughter, was playing on the carpet in front of them. She was a cheerful three-year-old with dark hair and Tony's eyes. Behind them, through an Edwardian leaded-glass window, was Hyde Park and the Russian Embassy. Beatles music was playing softly in the background.

'London is so cool. They really appreciate contemporary art,' Tony continued.

I hadn't seen Yoko and Tony since Tokyo. A few months after I left Japan, they returned to New York. I had already left the States for Europe so we had missed each other. Yoko had commenced her career as an artist in New York, and returned to the city with some exciting new pieces. She was becoming famous in the art world, doing performance pieces at venues like the Little Carnegie at Carnegie Hall on 57th Street.

I took another sip of the Earl Grey tea Jill had made for us all as Tony and I continued to catch up.

'How did you get to London?' Tony asked, through a haze of dope smoke.

'We brought our poetry review *Residu* here last year from Athens and never left.'

In the sitting room, Yoko and Jill were hitting it off. Yoko was so devoted to her work; it must have been comforting to get to know a woman who appreciated what she was doing. Jill painted and was involved with the underground art scene since her years at the Sorbonne in Paris, where she studied poetry. Jill had a gentleness about her. Even though she was deeply involved with the avant-garde, the hip culture, and consciousness expansion, she was still, underneath, a proper English lady. Three months has passed now since we lost David and as Jill and Yoko talked, I could see a light beginning to enter Jill's sad eyes.

We had just moved into the wonderful, lovely flat at Palace Court overlooking Hyde Park. It was a step-up after living in bed-sits and borrowed digs like Denbigh Close.

'How did you get to work for Stanley Kubrick? Man that is fucking cool.' Tony picked up Kyoko, who had come into the kitchen, and sat her on his lap.

'Through mutual friends of Arthur Clarke and Stanley Kubrick.'

Yoko, Tony, and Kyoko came by for Christmas dinner. Needing some wine, Yoko and I had gone down to the Bayswater Road to see if we could find somewhere open. It was a cold day and as we walked briskly along, I heard a voice across the street calling me.

'Dan! Hey, Dan!'

I turned to see my old friend from India, Peter Bendrey, standing outside the pub across the street. He still looked so young with a sparse boyish beard and light brown hair pulled back in a ponytail. He couldn't have been more than twenty-one or twenty-two at the time.

'Oh my God, Peter,' I said as we threw our arms around each other. I hadn't seen him since we left Srinagar in April of 1964 after our winter with Zina and Ronnie. When the spring thaws arrived in the Himalayas, I left for Tokyo and Peter went back down into India.

'How are you, man? You look great,' I said, with my hands still on his shoulders.

'Couldn't be better, mate. I'm just back from India. I didn't want to spend Christmas in Paris, so I pushed on and I just arrived. You look great, too.'

I introduced Peter to Yoko and we invited him to join us for Christmas dinner.

Hanover Gate Mansions

1967 was the transition year. Up till then all the new kids turning on and dropping out were imitating the hipsters and the beats. But in 1967 everything changed. You could look at it as before *Sergeant Pepper's Lonely Hearts Club Band* and after it. The Beat and hipster jargon was transforming into the new hippie-speak and baggy old turtlenecks sweaters, corduroys, and dishevelled hair were being replaced by kaftans, velvets, and beads. Just as The Beatles with *Sergeant Pepper* had transformed and liberated popular music, every aspect of society was being liberated. Draft cards were being burnt. Kids were turning on, growing their hair, and walking away from homes, schools, and jobs. They were descending on the Haight in San Francisco, the Village in New York, and cities all over Europe – London, Paris, Amsterdam, and Rome. It was a naïve and exciting time, full of an exhilarating energy and joy that only had a short time before the inevitable consequences of our experiments with individual freedom would start taking its toll.

Since our evening with Paul McCartney at John and Marianne's, we didn't have direct contact with any of the Beatles for over a year. All through 1967, I was still working as Stanley Kubrick's choreographer. *2001: A Space Odyssey* turned into a long project and after a few months, in addition to doing the choreography, I was starring in it. Stanley had convinced me to play the man-ape called Moonwatcher who picks up a bone and starts to use it as a weapon, beginning the long ascent from man-ape to man. I didn't know then that that moment in the film when I pick up that bone and throw it into the air would become one of the seminal moments in film history. I was just thrilled to be working with Stanley and making a lot of money doing something I loved. *2001* was big and way over budget. Even though we were shooting it in North London under a pall of great secrecy rumours abounded. I was getting all kinds of invitations by people who wanted to meet and talk with me.

Jill and I had comfortably settled into a spacious flat at 26 Hanover Gate Mansions. Hanover Gate was a row of Edwardian town house apartments just across from Regent's Park, in the centre of London. I was fast becoming a Londoner. We shared a whole floor with Yoko and Tony. Since that day at Palace Court, we had seen a lot of them. Tony found the apartments and we each decided to take one. Our two apartments made the whole floor and they were rapidly becoming a gathering spot for artists, poets, film people, as well as numerous hip types. I'll never forget my boyhood friend Henry Geldzaler, the head of 20th Century Art at the Metropolitan Museum in New York, standing in the living room with one of Jill's blond wigs on with a cigar in his mouth. The apartments were mildly elegant, big with high ceilings and wooden floors. There was a long balcony that ran along the front of the building. Yoko and Tony were doing Yoko's performance pieces and films. Jill and I were publishing the second edition of our poetry review *Residu.* I also had an antique stall on the Portobello Road, so our space was filled with Victorian and Chinese furniture and collectables. In contrast, Yoko and Tony kept their apartment completely bare. The floor was covered with neutral carpet, and there was no furniture except for a table and chairs in the kitchen and a bed. They had nothing on the white walls and no curtains.

Yoko and Tony made such an odd couple. Tony always seemed to be doing something. He took care of Kyoko and managed Yoko's career. Our apartment had become a hang-out as we had furniture, TV, and good dope. Yoko had a way of sitting with her eyes closed as though she was asleep. She was listening to everything, however, and opened her eyes now and then to say things

like, 'Can you borrow a fog machine from MGM for me to use?'
Tony and Kyoko watched TV and we all smoked dope and talked
about art, the hip scene, and our careers.

'At the Little Carnegie in New York, I was putting on this event
where the idea was that I would sit on a chair on the stage and not
move. The whole idea was that I would do absolutely nothing, but
the audience didn't know that.' Yoko was describing the work she
did in New York after we all left Tokyo. She, Tony, Jill and I were
sitting in our living room.

'One by one the audience members began to figure it out and
some were angry and some laughed, but they got up and left one
by one,' she continued with a smile on her face. 'I kept very still
and didn't move, but there was this one guy who refused to leave,
he just sat there quietly, too, very Zen.' We all laughed.

Yoko was doing a lot of shows and events. She had amazing
energy and single-mindedness. She was always working on another
project. Everything she did was uniquely hers. Her work had a
clean, artful simplicity about it, yet it was always intelligent and
made people think. She published a small book called *Grapefruit*,
which was full of her writings and drawings; she also gave performances, did events, and made films. At one point, she had a
large event in Trafalgar Square where she wrapped up one of the
lion statues in white cloth. Her career was really starting to take
off. She was becoming accepted as being in the vanguard of what
was happening in conceptual art.

What I liked most about her work is that, along with its Zen
simplicity, she always involved the audience. She had done a piece
at the Indica gallery where the audience was invited to climb a
white ladder leading to a small white canvas on the ceiling with a
magnifying glass hanging from it. If you looked through the glass,
you could see the word 'yes' in small letters on the canvas. It was
this piece that impressed John Lennon. He saw it at the Indica
Gallery when he met her there before the opening of her show.

As we talked, she wondered aloud if John Lennon is really that important. Tony emphatically reminded her who the Beatles were and who John was and he emphatically encouraged Yoko to pursue John as a patron.

It seems that everyone was smoking dope – It was everywhere. You smelled pot on the streets; there were references to it in songs and in the media; and at parties even the straight people were taking a puff.

I had been so busy working that I hadn't been able to get the time to go into rehab. I was doing everything I could to be able to function as normally as possible. In order to keep my dose from increasing, I had hired a private nurse to hold the heroin and disperse it to me daily. But addiction is a progressive disease. If you keep on using it just gets worse. Aside from the debilitating physical consequences of using intravenous heroin the psychological effects take their toll as well. Self esteem tanks and you live so much of your life deceiving yourself and others, there are relentless moral consequences.

I would lie awake at night and wonder how heroin had got such a devastating hold on me. I remembered how in India my innocent experiments with smoking opium had taken hold of me almost immediately. Like most addicts it filled a gaping hole I had in me that before the opium I hadn't realised was there. Like Pandora's Box, once that hole was uncovered there was no peace until I used some opium again. My short stay in the States was hell as I was afraid that if I used hard drugs I would end up in jail. In Athens, I could get opium in the drug stores but heroin was also easy to get and soon I was using it regularly.

In England, addicts registered with the Home Office and we received our drugs legally. It allowed us to avoid the withdrawal sickness and we were able to function almost normally and work. In spite of my nurse my dose of heroin kept creeping up and I needed more and more to stay normal. The larger doses led to

Lady Frankau also prescribing cocaine and methamphetamine to counteract the effects of the large amounts of heroin. The goal was to stabilise, so as to be prepared to come off when my work on *2001* was done at the end of 1967. This was easier said that done and I wanted to avoid going back into a cycle of unsuccessful detoxification sessions and cures. I wanted to stop being in and out of nursing homes and using again after each failed cure.

'Hi Bill, what are you doing out here?' Bill Burroughs was standing on a balcony from where he could monitor the entrance to Panna Grady's mansion near Hanover Gate across from Regent's Park. It was another Allen Ginsberg birthday bash. Birthday parties for Allen seemed to be getting bigger and wilder as the counter-culture exploded. Looking through the crowd, I had seen Bill's skinny figure alone out on the balcony in a suit and fedora and gone over to him. Looking like a private detective, he turned at me with a glum smile and said 'Hi.' Then with a grimace, he gestured to the crowd below coming in the main entrance.

'This is the safest place to be,' he muttered in his mid-western twang. 'This place is full of creeps and junkies. Look at all these kids, there is dope everywhere and when the cops come through that door down there I'm jumping out this window down behind those bushes over there and I'm out of here.'

'Yeah, there certainly are an awful lot of kids turning on now.'

Bill always had a dry humour that reminded me of my grand-father George who was also a Mid-westerner who looked a lot like Bill and had that same sense of humour.

As he kept an eye on the door, Bill and I talked about a little-known cure for heroin that he had taken. It was called the Apomorphine cure. The cure was not used very much outside of Russia and Scandinavia, so Bill gave me the name of some people to talk to and recommended a book by a Dr Dent called *Anxiety and its Treatment*.

Being an addict had been hell while working on *2001*. If I

stopped I'd be too sick to perform and going on using left me in constant fear of discovery. When I had to let go a young dancer who was helping me develop the man-apes, but wasn't suitable to play one, he told Kubrick that I was an addict. When Stanley found out, he was great. I explained to him I was a legally registered addict and that I was going to go back into rehab after the film was finished. He stuck by me, he needed me to finish the picture and I think he was fascinated to learn more about addicts. He would ask me questions like how often I shot up, how soon would I get sick if I didn't take it, and we discussed my plans for a cure. I told him about the Apomorphine cure and that I was looking for a copy of Dr Dent's book which was out of print. A couple of days later when I went into his office to discuss something about my choreography, he handed me a copy of the book.

'I bought two,' he said, 'one for you and one for me, I've been reading it, very interesting.'

Stanley was always devouring new information on just about anything. We would have conversations that covered a dizzying spectrum of subjects. I have always been like that too, I am endlessly fascinated by what ever swims into view. Never bored; never enough time.

John becomes Yoko's Patron

Yoko took Tony's advice and asked John to support her work. On October 11th, 1967 she put on a large show called *Half-a-Wind* at the Lisson Gallery in London. As Jill and I walked through the show, we saw that every piece was one-half of an object that had been cut in two.

To our amazement, John had put up enough money for Yoko to cut a real Ford sedan in half.

'I think John is becoming more than a casual patron,' I said to Jill as we looked at the Ford and tried to figure what it had cost.

'Oh, come on, Dan. She has many well-off patrons, look at Peggy Guggenheim,' said Jill.

'I don't know – a rock and roll star being this interested in a conceptual artist? I know he's the cultured Beatle, but I find it a bit surprising. Tony seems to be a bit more agitated than usual, too. Maybe I'm just imagining it. Whatever, it's a great show.'

This was a critical time of transition for me. Having just finished *2001*, I was ready to come off heroin. After many failed cures and nursing homes I was really desperate. I had to get clean. The experiment had turned into a nightmare. Somehow I had been able to complete *2001*, but I was worn out, tired, disillusioned and depressed. Jill and I were trying to have another child and here I was just another junkie. So on November 2, 1967, determined to finally free myself from the addiction; I started the Apomorphine cure that Bill Boroughs had recommended. In the West it was considered very radical, but it had helped Bill and was used success-fully in the Soviet Union. It was a kind of aversion therapy. Doctor Kelly put me in an apartment in Chelsea with private nurses who stayed with me all through the treatment. After a shot of

Apomorphine I was given a couple of shot glasses of whiskey. Each time it made me violently ill. Then a few hours later they did it again. I endured it for almost three days.

Pale and shaky I came home. I must have looked like a ghost after three days of convulsive vomiting and no food. Food was hard to keep down and I felt incredibly tired and empty. Sitting on the sofa on our living room I saw a tiny heroin pill in the pile of the rug. I just stared at it for an interminable time with an unbearable fear. Then like a zombie I picked it up to flush down the toilet. Just touching it and feeling it in my hand was suddenly exhilarating. My fear had turned to excitement and I felt helpless. That tiny pill had complete power over me and as I stared at it I knew I would use it. I was back dancing the terrible dance of death with heroin. Over the next few days I had devastating feelings of failure and sank deeper into despair, low self esteem and self loathing. Would I ever get clean? Be careful what you wish for, I was a terminal addict.

The Beatles were everywhere and into everything. They were seen in clubs every night, and all the groupies in town wanted to sleep with them. On December 4th, 1967 they opened a big clothing boutique at 94 Baker Street, on the corner of Paddington Street. They had given the art collective, The Fool, a whole lot of money to design and stock it with colourful sixties clothing. The Fool was a group of four designers that included the Dutch artist Simon Posthuma. They designed record sleeves, posters, and fashion for rock and roll artists.

Hanover Gate was at the top of Baker Street, close to the boutique. Jill and I watched it go up. It was a magnificently impractical testament to Sixties' London. Walking through it, we tried on the velvet and silk clothing. All the fashions were works of art. On the street, people stopped to stare at the outside of the building, which had been painted with swirling psychedelic murals. There were complaints from the local Conservative council.

2001 came out in the spring of 1968 and within a few weeks it had been recognised as one of Stanley's greatest films. At first people weren't sure what to make of it but soon the word got out that it was a 'trip movie'. The balconies smelt of pot and people saw it over and over again. But *2001* was so much more than that and over the years it has taken its place as one of the great movies of all time. The scene where I crush a skull with a bone and throw it in the air has come to be recognised as one of the classic moments in film history. I have become what Arthur Clarke called 'the most famous unknown actor in the world.'

Yoko and Ornette Coleman at the Albert Hall

'Dan, this is Ornette Coleman.' Yoko and the American jazz musician were standing at my door. They made a strange pair, he in a Nehru jacket and Yoko in her black sweater and pants. It was February 1968.

'Hi, it's great to meet you.' I ushered them in.

Yoko explained that Ornette was booked to perform at the Albert Hall but was having trouble getting a work visa.

'If anyone can help you get you a visa to perform in England, it's Dan. He produced the Albert Hall poetry reading,' Yoko said.

'I'm flattered, Yoko, but there were some others involved in putting that reading together.'

Looking at Ornette I said, 'it's almost impossible for American jazz musicians to get permission to perform in England without a reciprocal exchange where a British musician performs in the States.'

Yoko was excited and wouldn't take no for an answer. She had just performed with Ornette in Paris and she wanted people to see her as a singer as well as an artist.

'OK, I'll give it a try,' I said.

Although Ornette was best known as a jazz musician, Tony and I were able to get him a work visa by convincing the British Home Office that he was also a classical composer. We persuaded well-known music professors to write letters saying Ornette had written classical music. This was actually true, as some of his compositions had been performed by classical orchestras in the States.

On February 29, 1968 Ornette and Yoko held the concert. I helped them set up the Albert Hall with stadium seating like we did for the *Wholly Communion* poetry reading. The stage was in the centre of the auditorium where the boxing ring normally went. It took two frenetic weeks to get all the papers in order and the hall ready. Dave Izenson and Charlie Hayden played bass and Ed Blackwell was on drums. I drove Dave and his big bass to the hall in my little Mini. I still don't know how we squeezed it in.

It was a great event. I had never seen Yoko sing before and I was surprised by her style. It sounded completely unique. She and Ornette riffed all night. People seemed uncomfortable with her singing, which just sounded Japanese to me. Most people reacted negatively to it and didn't think it belonged at a jazz concert. Ornette recorded the evening and Yoko later used it as the B-side of her Plastic Ono Band album.

Yoko was seeing more and more of John and, as they became closer, Tony started to lose his cool. One day he knocked on our door. As I opened it, I could see he was agitated when he showed me a piece of paper he wanted Yoko to sign. It guaranteed him one-half of the profits from her work.

'Do you really think it would ever stand up, Tony?' I asked.

A short time later I was working in my studio when Jill came in saying. 'Dan, look out the window'.

'What is it?' I said, looking up from my desk.

'Just look, there down on the street in front of the building.'

Parked right by the entrance of Hanover Gate was John's Rolls Royce.

A few weeks later I was over at Tony and Yoko's. Tony was rummaging around in the closets, removing articles of clothing that were left. He pulled out a gorgeous black velvet, double-breasted coat that had come from the Apple boutique, out of a closet.

'Here, do you want it? I don't.' He was angry.

'Let me try it on.'

The jacket was soft and fitted perfectly. It buttoned up high on the chest and had a high Edwardian collar.

'I love it man are you sure?'

'Yeah, keep it,' he muttered as he continued to rummage around in the closet.

During the early spring of 1968 with our new baby coming and a career in pictures, I was desperate to stop using heroin but just couldn't. My failure after the Apomorphine treatment had left me very depressed. Every time I failed to come off heroin I sunk deeper into despair and self-loathing. After the release of *2001*, I was praised for my performance and choreography. I had become a movie star and choreographer with a hit and I was dead inside.

To supplement our income, I was still selling antiques in the Portobello Road market on Saturday mornings. I was also a pretty good photographer, so I was doing some fashion jobs and selling my photos to magazines.

Once again, I ran into Peter Bendrey on the street. He had just returned from India and moved in with us at Hanover Gate with a big sitar he was learning to play. He arrived like an angel of mercy and began to take care of us. Jill was very sick with another pregnancy and I was depressed and broken from battling my addiction.

'Why do we just keep running into each other?' I asked Peter as we sat in our kitchen smoking one of Peter's big cone-shaped joints and drinking tea.

'It must be destiny, man. I guess we are meant to spend time together. You know you completely opened up my head,' he said as he exhaled.

Peter took a job in a health food restaurant called Cranks and every night he brought us back healthy food to eat. He spent hours in the kitchen baking bread; he even built us some shelves.

Yoko and Peter became confidants as the John and Tony thing played out. I often saw them talking together. Peter was the perfect listener.

Yoko and John had definitely become an item. I didn't know all the details but Tony took Kyoko and left for the South of France. He must have been on reasonable terms with them since Yoko asked Peter to take money down to Tony and Kyoko. Peter couldn't get a flight to anywhere in France. It was May 1968 and there were major demonstrations taking place in Paris led by students. The streets were barricaded and the whole country seemed to have shut down. Peter had to fly to Turin in Northern Italy and rent a car. He filled up the trunk with cans of petrol since you couldn't buy any in France, and delivered the money to Tony.

Yoko Brings John to Tea

There was a knock on the door. It was late morning and Jill and I were nervously expecting John and Yoko. They were becoming inseparable. Jill and I had never met John. We had seen him at Allen Ginsberg's birthday party, and his Rolls was often parked out front to pick up Yoko, but this was our first meeting. We were nervous – he was a Beatle and they were pop royalty in London in those days. He was one of the most famous human beings in the world and he was stopping by to chat. Yoko said he wanted to meet me because of my role in *2001*. She was clearly in love with John, so we wanted to make him welcome.

'What do you serve a Beatle?' I asked Jill as I walked towards the door. 'Do I just roll a joint?' I said, as I fumbled for the doorknob.

'Don't be daft, he's British. We can't go wrong offering him a cup of tea,' she said. 'I'll just make a nice pot of Earl Grey.'

I opened the door and John and Yoko were standing there in front of the Edwardian birdcage elevator. They seemed to fit together as if there was a physical connection between them. John looked skinny and nervous. He was not at all imposing; he was wearing jeans, a jean jacket, and a T-shirt.

Yoko said something like, 'Dan and Jill, this is John.' She had a funny way of sucking in her breath after she spoke.

'It's great to meet you, come on in.' I said and we all went down the hall to the living room. John and Yoko settled on our oversized burgundy Chesterfield sofa. John looked even smaller perched there, and he was obviously nervous. It was as if he didn't belong in this world, just a stranger on a visit here.

'I'll just put the kettle on,' said Jill.

Jill's sensible English accent, as well as the act of starting to make the tea, seemed to put John at ease.

'So you were the ape in *2001*? That's really cool, must have been great working with Stanley Kubrick.' His Liverpudlian accent was delightfully disarming. We began to talk. It turned out that he was a major fan of *2001*. He seemed genuinely excited to meet me. As we all began to relax, I noticed that John had a way of lifting his head slightly, as if to see better through his glasses. I could also detect a physical awkwardness.

'Dan isn't just the ape in *2001*.' Yoko described some of the events I had been involved with, like the poetry reading and her concert with Ornette. She told him about *Residu*, my photography, and my mime background.

Soon the inevitable joint was rolled and we were all very comfortable. As I watched John, I began to understand why he and Yoko were attracted to each other. I knew John had started out at art school and always wanted to be an artist. I realised that Yoko was not just introducing her new boyfriend to two of her best friends; she was also exposing him to the hip art world. I could see John wanted to be cool and accepted. Yoko was his guide, his entrée.

We talked about a lot of things. Outside our window, the London of 1968 was a swirl of energy and change. It was fuelled by a dynamo of music, ideas, politics, drugs, and most of all, the dreams we all had. John talked about how Yoko had helped him realise that he could use his immense popularity to fulfil some of those dreams.

'That's so cool, man,' I said. 'As we sit here smoking a joint, all around us a new world is forming that we all believe will replace the tired and narrow old one. To be such a major part of that change must feel incredible.' John looked almost embarrassed.

'Yeah, this is more than kids smoking dope and listening to rock and roll,' I continued.

'But it's all those kids who are listening to the Beatles that we can reach,' said John.

'When John talks about peace or says the war is over, millions of fans hear it,' continued Yoko.

Suddenly it all seemed to fall into place. Her successes in the art worlds of Tokyo, New York, and London were just a beginning. She and John together were going to continue what she was doing and that would help John become something greater than he was. John, for his part, was going to help her with her music and move her from the art world into the mainstream.

'And all this is happening because I was bored one day and went to the Indica Gallery looking for sex,' said John.

After we all stopped laughing, Jill said, 'I'll make some more tea.' But John and Yoko had to leave, so we saw them out.

Things Start to Get Heavy

her hair falling caught the light
and threw it back to me
I caught it too
jester juggler
junkie

Dan Richter – Athens 1964

Change was in the air everywhere. The flower-power-hippie movement had reached a critical mass and young people were taking
Tim Leary's advice, 'turning on, tuning in, and dropping out.'
The energy and freedom mixed with racial and social upheavals
created a dizzying chaos. In the middle were John and Yoko,
emblematic of that change.

All around us things were heating up. The peaceful scruffy
hippies with flowers and peace symbols on their Volkswagen
vans began to mutate into intense young radicals demanding
change at demonstrations. A hard side began to emerge; Martin
Luther King and Bobby Kennedy were assassinated, the Vietnam
War had become the longest war in US history, and students at
colleges were protesting and taking over buildings like they did at
Columbia University. During the last few days of August 1968 at
the Democratic Convention in Chicago, hippies, anti-war radicals,
and Black Panthers protesting the war were beaten up by police
while the whole world watched on TV.

On September 14, 1968, our son Sacha was born at the Charing
Cross Hospital. He was a beautiful baby. Jill and I both felt we
were really getting back on track. Now that the baby had arrived,
Peter was aching to return to India. He needed to get going before

the passes closed for the winter. One night before he left he and I were talking about John and Yoko.

'If she hadn't come along, he probably wouldn't have made it. She pulled him out of a spin he was in,' said Peter.

'Well, I haven't really seen that much of him, but I can certainly see that she has had a real effect on him. They're doing all these new projects,' I said.

'He had a world weariness and cynicism in him that is disappearing. It's Yoko,' he said.

We said goodbye to Peter. He told us later that when he was boarding the ferry to Europe, he noticed a car with Pakistani license plates. He asked the two guys in it for a ride and ended up going with them all the way to Multan in Northern Pakistan, via Zahadan in Southern Iran and then across the Baluchi desert.

Now that Yoko was part of John's world of rock and roll elite, she started to dress the part. She and John were constantly in the spotlight. Up until then, she always wore black jeans and a black sweater. She was the embodiment of conceptual simplicity with her black garb, minimal art, and bare home. Yoko considered Jill and I part of the 'beautiful people' with our silks and velvets and other sixties affectations.

She began to borrow clothes from Jill. She would stop by and the two of them would look through Jill's things trying to decide what would look good on her. Yoko really needed her own things so Jill went round London to buy clothing for her. She found some really lovely stuff, gossamer-thin long dresses and robes covered with Indian block-printed designs. Both Yoko and Jill wore headbands of the same material. They were developing a hip sixties look with an Asian flair. Yoko was very enthusiastic and the stuff looked great on both of them.

Yoko and John were getting involved in heavier drugs like heroin. This was very dangerous since they were spokespersons for the hip revolution and were falling under greater scrutiny from the authorities. At this time they were changing from being an aspect of the Beatle phenomenon to counter-culture activists and it put them on a collision course with Richard Nixon.

The first ominous sign of the problems to come happened on October 18, 1968. They were arrested for possession of hashish during a midnight raid at an apartment Ringo had loaned them. The arresting officer was the notorious Sergeant Pilcher, who had previously arrested Donovan and the Rolling Stones. It was indicative of the hassles they would get for being together and saying what they really thought. This arrest would be the basis of the deportation order used later to try to get them out of the States when they moved to New York.

Through all of the travails they were experiencing, one thing was very clear – John and Yoko were really in love. Anyone who knew them could see it. The press might be ranting that Yoko was breaking up the Beatles or that she had John under her sway, but the fact was they met and fell in love. They were inseparable. It was as though they were breathing each other's air or thinking each other's thoughts. Whatever one did, the other wanted to do. John hung on Yoko's every word. He wanted to be a conceptual artist and Yoko wanted to be a rock and roll star. This, of course, presented numerous practical difficulties. The juggernaut of the Beatles was in trouble. John and Paul were drifting into what could become a messy divorce. Most of the Beatles insiders were treating Yoko terribly. They saw her as a gold digger whose assertive ways were exacerbating the problems the Beatles were having staying together. She was not acting like just another Beatles' wife. As a result, she was openly insulted in front of John.

The Beatles had become much more than musical stars. They touched every aspect of culture and society all around the world. They were millionaires and cultural icons, and at the heart of it all, their music was the soundtrack for a world that was changing irrevocably all around us. Everyone wanted to hear their opinions on everything. There were drug references in their latest songs, and every day on TV, you could see them around London in flamboyant hippie clothes, being interviewed about peace, the Maharishi, or some other aspect of sixties culture.

The whole world had seen the Beatles on TV the year before on their way to visit the Maharishi in India. For guys who have travelled all around the world, they seemed naïve and gullible, falling prey to each new fad and idea that surfaced. The Maharishi had become the latest fad in Indian gurus and things spiritual. Because of the time I had spent in India, I was very suspicious of those gurus who want to be seen with rock stars. It seemed to me they were more interested in fame and money than nirvana.

Back in the States, things were going from bad to worse as the war continued to escalate and on 5 November 1968, Nixon won the presidential election.

Christ, You Know It Ain't Easy

We all hoped 1969 would be a more peaceful year than 1968 was. John and his wife Cynthia had divorced in September and Yoko and Tony's divorce went through in February. John and Yoko were travelling and doing so much together that we didn't see Yoko as much as when she lived next door. Even so Jill and Yoko were always talking on the telephone and Jill was still helping Yoko buy clothes.

'Dan, come look. It's Yoko.'

On March 20th Jill was sitting in the living room, watching the evening news on the TV. There were pictures of John and Yoko getting married in Gibraltar.

'My god, look at that miniskirt,' I said. Yoko had on this short white wedding dress and a big white hat. John was wearing a baggy white suit.

'They look so happy,' said Jill. And they did. It looked like they had overcome all the opposition and ridicule that was dumped on them and they really were committed and in love.

A few days later in room 902, the Presidential Suite at the Amsterdam Hilton, Yoko and John conducted a 'bed-in' for peace. They invited the world to share their honeymoon with them as they spent a week in bed promoting peace. From their bed they were conducting interviews with the press, having friends visit, drawing pictures, and singing songs. This was performance art taken to a new level. Now that they were married they had a new freedom. Yoko was no longer the 'Japanese actress who is breaking up the Beatles,' she was married to John Lennon and they had an agenda completely separate from the Beatles.

On May 1, 1969, hoping a geographical cure would help my drug problem, Jill and I took Sacha and went back to the States to stay at my home in Provincetown. P'town was a summer resort, art colony, and fishing village on the tip of Cape Cod in Massachusetts. My parents lived there full-time and the prospect of sun-washed dunes and the laid-back art colony atmosphere seemed like a positive change from the drugged-out, high pressure life of London. No such luck, it wasn't. Drugs and the hippie thing had invaded there too. Desperate to earn a living, I took a job as a cook in a friend's restaurant and one of the cooks working next to me was using heroin. I had jumped right out of the frying pan into the fire. I was dejected and humiliated. I had gone from movie star to cook to support my family and was shooting dope again. Worst of all, heroin was really illegal in the States and I had my parents there to witness my distress. I was demoralised and becoming desperate. After only a month and a half, we left to avoid the draconian US drug laws. We returned to London with our eleven-month-old baby Sacha and were staying on Alex Trocchi's sofa. I started using heroin regularly again. Lady Frankau had died a few months before we left for the States and now, without her and having been away, I had lost my registered status with the Home Office. I had to buy the drug illegally. Though not as dangerous as in the States, that still made me a criminal. Worse than that, it was hard to get pharmaceutical heroin so I never knew what quality of junk I was using.

Alex's fourth floor apartment on Observatory Gardens was still a literary gathering place. Regulars like R. D. Laing, Bill Borroughs and Michael X were often there. Allen Ginsberg and Robert Creeley stopped by when they were in town. There was always another pair of literary feet climbing the stairs to Alex's eyrie to smoke a joint, use some horse, or just have a cup of tea and discuss the hip literary gossip.

The heroin I was getting through Alex was mostly 'Chinese'. It was nasty stuff, a yellow brown powder in tin foil. Alex and I would cook it up and shoot it, then pray that the batch was really horse and wouldn't kill us.

'This is "Tiger" Dan, it's supposed to be really good stuff.' Alex would croon in his thick Scottish brogue. 'Just take a wee bit first to see how it feels. If you're alright in five minutes, you can shoot the lot,' he leant over the bubbling brown goo in the spoon.

The despair I felt was soul-crushing. All those cures, promises, plans, and here I was again, just a junkie playing Russian roulette.

Jill was talking to Yoko on the phone about our predicament and Yoko had an idea. She invited us to visit her at a Beatles recording session at the Abbey Road Studios. When we got there we were ushered into the control room of studio 3 where John and the other Beatles were working on their new *Abbey Road* album. John was very friendly, stopping what he was doing to say Hi. He introduced us to the others. There was Ringo, George, and Paul sitting around George Martin at the consul listening to the play-back of what they had just recorded. We had never met Ringo and George before. Both appeared mildly amused and seemed quite friendly as we said hello. I don't know if Paul remembered us as he was obviously pissed at John for having Yoko's friends disturb the recording that was already marred from his point of view by Yoko using the studio as an infirmary.

'Yoko's over there having a little rest,' John said, pointing through the control room window to the other side of the studio where Yoko was ensconced in a really big brass bed. She and John had been in a car accident in Scotland and she was still recuperating.

Things had settled down a bit with Tony and Cynthia and they planned a trip to Scotland to visit John's Aunt. They took Kyoko and John's five-year-old son Julian with them. The accident happened while they were up there. They were all in a little white car in the town of Golspie with John driving. Both John and Yoko needed stitches and Julian and Kyoko were badly shaken up. The car was totalled. John and Yoko had the twisted remains mounted on a block of concrete in the garden of Tittenhurst Park, the home they were buying in Ascot. You could still see blood on it.

To help Yoko recover, while the Beatles were recording, John had arranged for the large bed for her to lie in. Yoko was all in white, covered in white bedclothes and crocheting with white yarn.

Paul was glowering in icy silence.

It felt weird to be sitting on the bed talking to Yoko while the Beatles were working across the studio. I couldn't help thinking that those guys were making rock and roll history, while I was sitting on this bed in the middle of the Abbey Road studio, handing Yoko a small white packet.

A few weeks later Jill was on the phone with Yoko again. They were having another talk about our precarious situation. Yoko had an idea. John and his ex-wife Cynthia's mansion called Kenwood was empty. It was in the exclusive community of St George's Hill in Weybridge, just south of London, and they needed someone to keep an eye on it. We could live there for the time being. This would solve our housing problem and John's need to have someone at Kenwood.

They sent John's white Rolls Royce to pick us up from Alex Trocchi's.

'Dan, what's going to happen to us now?' Jill looked at me with ten-month-old Sacha in her arms. We were driving through the south of London, broke and desperate in a white Rolls Royce owned by the world's greatest rock star. Les Anthony, an ex-Welsh Guardsman who was John and Yoko's chauffeur, was driving. Dressed in a black suit, he was a large sullen man with jet-black hair and a swarthy complexion.

'He's creepy,' Jill whispered to me as she saw him catching glimpses of us in the rear view mirror. She nestled in tighter to me.

'Don't worry, darling, he probably just hates all of Yoko's friends.' Yoko was still considered an interloper by most of the people around the Apple office. Everyone treated her politely, but her profound influence over John was considered a source of the problems the Beatles were having staying together.

'Ya gonna stay long?' Les muttered, as we pulled up to an immense solid wooden gate in a high wall surrounding John's mini estate in London's stockbroker belt.

'Beats me,' I said.

Les got out and inserted a red plastic card in a slot and slowly the big gate rumbled open. We wound up the drive and came to a stop in front of the house.

'Oh my God, Dan, where are the doors?' John's quirky sense of humour was evident everywhere – the entry way was all walls made of mirrors.

'You've got to push here,' said Les, as one of the mirrors swung and became a door. 'Follow me,' he said as he grudgingly carried our bags up some stairs.

'We can't stay here forever,' Jill said, looking out of the window of the enormous empty bedroom at the rolling lawns of this gated enclave. The room was empty apart from a gigantic bed and a few large tea caddies filled with assorted Beatle memorabilia and personal stuff. 'Jill, come in here, look at this.' I had found a gigantic walk-in closet full of John's old clothing. The colours and materials were vivid. Silks, velvets, brocade – some strangely familiar as if I had seen them in publicity photos or paparazzi snaps. We tried things on as Sacha played among scores of exotic shoes and Beatle boots on the floor.

'These jackets look like they're from *Sgt Pepper*,' said Jill as she and Sacha waded through the clothing.

As I watched Jill and Sacha playing in this rock and roll grave-yard, I wondered how we had arrived at this point. I loved them so much and I felt so helpless. It was as though forces that were completely beyond our control were sweeping us along. The great experiment with absolute freedom that had characterised the last half of the sixties had produced a tumbling chaos. It seemed to have all degenerated into demonstrations, violence, drugs, and rock and roll.

The following day I heard the sound of a car coming up the drive. I looked through the open window, it was the white Rolls. Soon I could hear Les rummaging around in the rooms below. He clearly resented us as friends of the interloper Yoko. He was also pissed off that we were at Kenwood. He had had the place to himself since John and Yoko left it. He swam in the pool.

'I had to feed the cats.' Les was standing at the door, more humorous than ominous with his hair wet and a bit awry from the swim. Yoko was concerned that he was using Weybridge as a personal retreat. Somehow Kenwood had collected a gaggle of cats, mostly strays.

'Hey man, we can feed the cats; you don't have to worry about them. Just make sure you leave plenty of food,' I said.

His forehead creased as he realised he had one less reason to come by.

On August 9, 1969, the first of the Manson murders took place in Los Angeles. We were watching the news of the first victims, Roman Polanski's wife Sharon Tate and some of her friends in Los Angeles. The murders made Jill very edgy. What really brought it home to us was that we had met Roman at a dinner at Stanley and Christiane Kubrick's two years before and really hit it off with him. We were alone in this cavernous mock-Tudor estate that was known as John Lennon's house. It was creepy.

The following day, the next murder took place in Los Angeles. *Helter Skelter,* the name of a Beatles song, was written in blood on the walls by members of the Manson commune who had committed these terrible crimes. When we saw this, I started to become nervous, too.

'A maniac could break in looking for John and end up killing us,' said Jill, who was really scared.

The whole world had seemed to shift on its axis. The vision of absolute freedom we had all wanted to live by seemed to be turning on us. Rejecting the square world and cutting loose into this great sea of freedom had spawned more than we had bargained for. The reality was that drugs and violence were everywhere. I had an ongoing problem with heroin. I needed to find it daily, not just for me, but now for John and Yoko too. I had become everyone's source. I took the train into London every day to look for work and buy heroin for myself and for John and Yoko. Jill and Sacha were alone for long periods.

Meanwhile, John and Yoko were moving into their new eighty-five-acre estate in Ascot, Tittenhurst Park. The house was surrounded by large expanses of lawn and mown fields with stately trees that an earlier owner enamoured with dendrology had planted. There were magnificent specimens of trees from all over the world. Great walls of rhododendron, camellias and azalea rose scores of feet into the air.

There was plenty of room at Tittenhurst, so Yoko and John invited us to join them. The Manson thing had scared all of us. Yoko and Jill were very close and I was getting us dope. It was a good solution for all of us.

The problem was, that in finding refuge, we were also becoming inextricably involved in Yoko and John's lives. They had started to ask my opinion on some of the new projects they were initiating. They had a vision of using Ascot as a base to free themselves from the Apple office and John's Beatle past. They wanted to make their own records and films through which they could speak to the whole world about peace and the exciting new social ideas that were erupting all around us. They thought that Jill and I could be helpers on their quest. Once again in my life, I was being drawn toward a job I had not looked for. They already had an assistant,

Anthony Fawcett. Anthony was a skinny, bespectacled, nervous fellow in a white suit. He was from the art world rather than the world of rock and roll. Lacking in hip credentials, one couldn't imagine him smoking a joint. My reputation as a guy who had a knack for doing things everyone else thought couldn't be done was drawing me into Yoko and John's hip renaissance.

This attention was both good and bad for me. I had found a small part in *The Revolutionary*, a feature film starring Jon Voight. I was looking for movie work and I was hoping I could get my career back on track again. The problem was, of course, the heroin, that 800-pound gorilla that demanded my complete attention. As long as it had me in its grip, I would not have much time for anything else. It devoured all our money, our health, and constantly compromised my ability to take care of Sacha. I knew I was just biding time before the next disaster but, with the eternal denial of the addict, I saw Tittenhurst as a potential refuge. I was putting off kicking horse and using John and Yoko as a means to pay for the heroin and to give me a safe haven while I was still using.

On Friday, August 22, wearing a pair of rubber Wellington boots, I clunked in on all the Beatles sitting like morose pop demigods in a room off the gardens. They had come to Ascot for a photo shoot to promote *Abbey Road*. It was one of their last meetings together and the atmosphere was very tense. Paul and John were arguing over everything. Apple, their company, was haemorrhaging money. Paul had being telling the others what to do, particularly during recordings and John was pissed off at him and disillusioned about being a Beatle. He wanted an American named Allen Klein, with a reputation for being a tough music industry negotiator, to be the Beatles manager. Paul wanted his father-in-law, Lee Eastman, to have the job. George and Ringo went along with John and agreed to Klein becoming the manager. They seemed caught in the middle of the fight between John and Paul. The Beatle dream was just about over.

Being around Yoko and John all the time, I was beginning to understand a lot more about their relationship. Yoko was John's protector. In exchange, she had his total support. It was like an unspoken deal they had. They were completely and totally inseparable. They seemed to have this invisible radar between them so that as they moved and spoke there was an illusion that they were almost one person.

Sometimes Yoko appeared downstairs at Ascot without John, but it was always only to take care of some bit of business. He sat up in his room, apart from the world, with Yoko as his lover, attendant, teacher, and prime minister. I was starting to see that they had come together because each seemed to have a deep and driving need that the other could fill, and as each gave the other what was needed, a compact was formed and they were completely in love. The relationship had advanced so that Yoko was always there between John and the world. If the world saw or heard from him, Yoko was always beside him. She amended his statements, explained policy, and held his hand. He always put Yoko forward as an equal part of the whole that made up John and Yoko. From early in their relationship, people had attacked her viciously. John was deeply hurt and offended and he vehemently defended her. He had discovered that she was willing to be his foil. Imagine how effective for his purposes of breaking up the Beatles it was for him to always have Yoko present at recordings and meetings. This, of course, increased the howls of derision directed at her. They were not just victims in all this – Yoko's presence can be seen as a clever strategy used by John to achieve independence from the Beatles and his Beatle image. John didn't get to the top of the heap by just having some genius and a lot of luck; he was also very smart and extremely shrewd. But at the same time, Yoko and John were deeply wounded by these attacks, yet they fed on the energy and publicity they produced.

Yoko was changing. At Hanover Gate, she seemed to want

nothing but her art. Her clothes were always the same, utilitarian. Her apartment had no furniture, no curtains, and nothing on the walls. Clothes, furniture, and TV were not important. My recurring image of Yoko was of her all in black, sitting on her floor with her back against the bare wall. She was bathed in the stark light coming through the large, curtainless Edwardian windows.

Now Yoko was transforming into a rock star. There was something slightly incongruent about her dressing and acting this new role. Just as John was doing conceptual art, she was becoming a rock and roll singer and composer. Her singing was not going over well. She had a way of wailing when she sang that belongs in a Japanese temple and not on a rock stage. The word 'yowl' was used to describe it. John would not hear a word of criticism. The more she sang, the more the people at Apple couldn't stand her. To them, she was not only an interloper but a terrible singer to boot.

John saw her very differently. John saw a brilliant conceptual artist whose radical use of traditional Japanese singing techniques was bringing new forms and innovations to the rock idiom. Time has proved John mostly right, but back then the world was very much against Yoko.

A few days later after the Beatles photo shoot I was walking with John and Yoko in the garden when they had their first meeting with their head gardener Frank.

'We only want white and black flowers.' Yoko was speaking to Frank who was the classic English gardener – tweed jacket, wellington boots, and a tie, quite proper and completely confused by the new owners of the estate.

'Pardon, m'am, did you say only white and black flowers?'

'Yes, we don't want any colour at all, just pure white and black.' Yoko was quite firm. Frank looked over to John for help.

'Do you have a problem with that?' asked John. I was amused as I watched Frank struggle with the fact that his ordered domain was under assault by this strange Japanese woman and her rock star husband.

'Not at all, Mr Lennon . . . uh . . . I'm sure we can find some lovely white flowers, but black might be difficult.'

'There are some very dark tulips that look black. I'm sure you can find some other kinds, too,' said Yoko.

I was trying not to laugh. The four of us continued walking and discussing the changes Yoko and John required. Life at Tittenhurst was going to be fun.

It's Only Rock 'n' Roll

Bob then invited The Beatles to a game of tennis on the Forelands Farm courts. 'I'll play on condition nobody really knows how,' quipped John and, as Bob and John teamed up against Ringo and George, Patti Harrison giggled: 'This was the most exclusive game of mixed doubles in the world . . . ' The game ended at 5.30, and Dylan piled into a white van along with Sara, Ringo, Maureen, and me for the five mile drive to the festival site. We joked all the way.

Al Aronowitz from 'Bob Dylan and the Beatles',
Volume One of the Best of the Blacklisted Journalist
www.blacklistedjournalist.com

'Do you have a large flat lawn with enough space for me to land my helicopter?'

'Gosh, I think so. There's acres of park land and a lot of it is lawn.'

It was August 31, 1969 and I was talking on the phone to the pilot of the helicopter that John and Yoko had chartered to take us down to a big concert on the Isle of Wight. I was about to get my first real introduction to the world of rock and roll. Up until now I had only spent time around John. But now he had asked Jill and me to join him and Yoko on a trip to see Bob Dylan. Bob and Sarah Dylan had rented the large Forelands Farm and had invited John and Yoko to come down to see Bob and The Band in concert. Dylan was returning after a long convalescence following his motor-cycle accident. Ringo and Maureen Starkey, George and Patti Harrison, and numerous other rock heroes like Keith Richard and their entourages were going to be there as well.

'If you can give me a space clear of trees and just lay the sheet out flat, I'll see it and I can bring the chopper down.'

'How will you find us?'

'Piece of cake, mate, I just look at the map and follow the roads.'

I was beginning to understand the nature of the life of a major celebrity.

As the helicopter lifted off from Tittenhurst, Jill and Yoko were clearly nervous. It was tiny and had windows that created a glass bubble all around us. John had travelled on so many choppers, planes, limos, etc. in his life that he seemed completely in place. I was carrying one of the new Sony reel-to-reel videotape cameras that John had let me use. It was a new technology back then. This was the first time I had used a camera that allowed you to capture video on tape. I was so obsessed with taping that I was too busy to be concerned.

'Can you fly lower?' We were over the water heading south toward the Isle of Wight and I was filming the water racing by.

'No problem, mate,' said our pilot, dropping right down over the waves.

'Dan, stop it, you're going to get us killed,' Jill shouted over the sound of the rotor. Yoko leaned in closer to John.

Forelands Farm was large and posh. In a field by the main house, someone had put out bed sheets for us, and for Ringo and Maureen who were coming in at the same time in their own helicopter. Keith Richard had arrived and George and Patti had been there with Bob all week. Bob was rehearsing with The Band in a large barn. John had given me the acetate of the yet-to-be released *Abbey Road* album, which he intended to play for everyone.

The word 'farm' was a bit of a misnomer as Forelands was really a small luxurious estate.

We were all standing or sitting in a large living room when Bob and Sara came down a set of stairs *en famille*. Sara, an ex-model and Playboy Bunny, had a baby in her arms. She was pregnant and it was just starting to show. Bob looked shy and a bit chubby. It was eerie to meet this guy who had created the sound track for a lot of my life. I remembered staying up all night in Paris listening to *Don't Think Twice, It's All Right* a few hours before I left in the rain to hitchhike to India. This quiet family man standing in front of me was the who had made my teeth ache night after night as I listened, demented, to *Mr Tambourine Man*, high on cocaine in London.

'Hi, I'm Bob.'

Bob seemed shy, surrounded by John and Yoko, Ringo, George, Keith Richard, the guys from The Band, and all the other stars. They were treating him like royalty among royalty, like someone very special.

In this environment, what struck me immediately was how rich they all were. Everyone had their own entourage and constant security. There were business managers, agents, publicists, A & R people, drivers, personal assistants, buddies, dope dealers, spouses, children, hair dressers, dress makers, stylists, psychics, etc. There always seemed to be so many people around and everyone was focused on their particular star.

Famous rock stars are definitely apart from regular people. They have a quality of otherness about them and though they look, talk, and seem like us, they are different. The stars in this living room at Forelands were all so famous and had such defined public images that who they really were was somehow insignificant.

In the midst of all the chaos, John, Yoko, Jill, and I arrived at the venue. It was hours after Bob and The Band were originally scheduled to go on. A disorganised mass of cars, vans and people scrambled towards the muddy site that seemed like something out of Dante. Mal Evans, the Beatles' road manager, was there and, like a big benevolent bear, moved us through the crowd to seats a few rows back from the stage.

Finally Bob came out, seeming fragile and pudgy in a white suit.

I had never seen him with an electric guitar before. He and The Band began an electric set to the cheers and admiration of the fans and the rock and roll royalty.

On the day after the concert I had a call to be on the set of *The Revolutionary*, so Jill and I flew back with George and Patti. It was a bit awkward at first. We were used to being tolerated as 'Yoko's friends', but they were very friendly and soon put us at ease.

Back at Tittenhurst, my rock education continued. I was beginning to understand John's love of classic rock and roll. He always acknowledged his debt to the pioneers of the form. He was invited to the Toronto Rock and Roll Revival and decided he would perform with his and Yoko's newly named Plastic Ono Band. He was very excited about all the performers who were going to be there: Chuck Berry, Little Richard, Jerry Lee Lewis, Gene Vincent, Bo Diddley, and Junior Walker & the All-Stars. There would be some contemporary stars, too, like The Doors and Alice Cooper. John invited Jill and I along too.

On September 13, 1969, John, Yoko, Jill, Eric Clapton, bassist Klaus Voorman, drummer Alan White, and I boarded a plane for Toronto. John was working with Klaus, Alan, and Eric on the Plastic Ono Band recordings. Klaus was an old friend of all the Beatles from way back to their Hamburg days. Of medium build, Klaus had a light-coloured beard and a poised and friendly air about him. He was the artist who created the line drawings on the cover of the Beatles' *Revolver* album. Alan was playing drums when Ringo wasn't available. I knew Eric's work from Cream and I was excited to talk with him. He was soft-spoken, quietly intelligent, and had a boy-like quality about him. John rounded up the band to run hastily over some songs in the back of the plane. As I sat with Eric, we talked about guitars, music, and the rigours of rock and roll travel.

'Always loosen the strings of the guitar when you take it on a plane,' he explained, as he put his guitar back in its case.

Allen Klein, who had become the Beatles new business manager, met us at Toronto airport; he had his twelve-year-old daughter Robin with him. He and John talked hurriedly about business and the growing dispute with Paul as we navigated through the airport. John was optimistic about what Allen could do for the Beatles. He had just completed a successful re-negotiation of their contracts with EMI for Canada, Mexico, and the USA that would result in a big increase in revenue for them. The problem was that John was tired of the whole Beatle thing and under the new contract they had to release at least two albums per year until 1976.

Outside the arrivals building, we split into groups and climbed into a fleet of limousines. John motioned for Jill and I to stay close as we slipped into one of the limos. I was beginning to see John's expertise in touring as a famous rock and roll star. On the ride from the airport to the University of Toronto's Varsity Stadium, John's feelings about touring resurfaced. He talked about the fear and exhilaration of moving fast, surrounded by the chaos and madness of Beatlemania.

'It got to the point where we didn't even have to tune our instruments. The shouting and screaming was so loud no one could hear us playing. I remember one concert in Tokyo – instead of singing "I want to hold your hand", I was singing something like "I want to fuck your ass". No one knew.' I saw a sadness and frustration in his face. 'It was crazy. In Manila, we were sitting on the tarmac waiting to take off and Brian had a paper bag full of the cash they had given us. The police came on the plane and demanded we pay some sort of tax. Brian had to reach in the bag and pay them some of the cash before we could take off.' Maybe being a Beatle had its drawbacks.

As we approached the stadium, I got a taste of Beatlemania when the gate the driver took us to was not open. The teeming fans were trying to break into the limo or turn it over. John covered Yoko with his body and I covered Jill. This was what John meant when he talked about the scary quality of travelling as a Beatle. The limo was literally rocking up and down and from side to side. The faces pressing on the windows were grotesque. The gate finally opened and we entered the bowels of the stadium.

'I want to put a speaker on our limo at Ascot that will roar like a lion,' said John as he and I tried to reassure Yoko and Jill.

Inside the stadium the chaos was almost as bad, but at least we were protected from the crowds. The police and security were very nervous, the atmosphere was edgy. We were escorted to a private dressing area.

The rocker from the golden years of the fifties, Gene Vincent, pushed through the door and limped in to see John. Gene was dressed in black leather and his limp was from a bad car accident. He was swarthy, a little stocky, and John was clearly pleased to see a 'real' rock and roll star. Gene looked pretty messed up and the conversation soon turned to dope. John wanted some blow before he went on.

'Richard's got some. I'm sure he'd give me some for you, man,' he said to John, referring to Little Richard.

Gene came back a few minutes later with something that he claimed was cocaine in a little white and green plastic capsule. 'Give it to Dan,' said John. On inspection the 'cocaine' looks suspiciously like speed, but we tried some anyway.

'This is shit, man,' I muttered as we were taking off. 'I bet he just got this from some fan.'

When it came time to play, John was throwing up in the bathroom. I couldn't tell if it was nerves, heroin withdrawal or the lousy dope. I later learnt that he was always sick before a performance. As he, Yoko, and the band started to go to the stage, John told Jill and I to stay right beside them. He told us to go with them onto the stage for safety, and to make sure we didn't get separated.

As we jostled through the backstage crowds and approached the stage, I noticed D. A. Pennebaker and Ricky Leacock filming a documentary on a hand-held camera. John stepped out onto the stage and the crowd exploded. The force of the energy was palpable. It was like a force of nature, big beyond control, terrifying. I was stunned. I was standing on stage beside John Lennon and Eric Clapton as they performed. Thank god I had my 35mm Nikon.

Hare Krishna, Hare Rama

Back at Tittenhurst, life was settling down. Jill, Sacha, and I were living in the big house in some rooms above the kitchen.

'I want the transom window over the front door to be clear glass with "This was not here" engraved on it.' Yoko was explaining how she wanted the front door area designed. It would look minimalist but very elegant. The white door was covered by a white portico supported by two Ionic columns. The door had a slim, clear window on each side of it to light the entry hall. There were two weathered concrete Victorian busts on each side of the door.

I was having fun helping John and Yoko make a plan to renovate the house and divide it into a living area for them with the rest of the house a work area. John wanted his own recording studio. Then we realised they would need offices with a telex and copying machines, an editing room, projection room, a colour dark room and archive space.

Yoko and I had a meeting in the room above the kitchen that we were turning into an editing room. Yoko spoke in a lowered voice, as though the discussion we were having was just between us. She asked me to work for them, taking over much of what their assistant Anthony Fawcett did. She told me they were going to phase him out once he had completed some of the work he was doing on their art projects.

The idea of officially working for them was too weird. I just couldn't see myself as a member of a sycophantic entourage.

'Yoko, I don't want a job.'

She persisted and I finally I told her, 'OK, but on the condition that I'm not officially working for you and I don't want to be paid.' We were already getting a place to stay, food, and dope. I preferred to see the time with them as a respite, a port in the storm where my family and I could be safe while I regrouped and figured out how to get a handle on my drug problem.

A few days later I was talking to John in his and Yoko's bedroom.

'George has this guy Eddie Veale building a studio for him over at Friar Park,' John said. Friar Park was George's 120-room mansion a few miles away at Henley-on-Thames.

'He is one of the best sound engineers in England. I want him to build our studio.'

This was going to be a big job; I got the feeling that I would be spending a lot of time with Eddie.

We decided that John and Yoko's living area would be all white with white carpet. The work areas would be covered with black carpet and the walls would be covered with a thick gray board that you could pin things to. All the original wood and doors would be stripped and left natural. The work area would have a rectangular electrical conduit along the walls that we could pull cable through. The switch plates and hardware would be stainless steel. We planned to tear down a lot of the walls so that the smaller eighteenth-century space could be replaced with spacious rooms. The kitchen area would be completely gutted and a large modern stainless steel kitchen would replace it.

Above the kitchen we had already installed a Steenbeck film-editing table and next to the kitchen we had started to clear space so we could build John's studio, control room, dark room, and archives. In the rooms where Jill and I were staying, we would put a sauna. There was a row of four cottages where there once was a blacksmith's forge. These would be renovated; two would be combined for Jill and me to live in. There was a lot of work to do, and it all had to be done while records were being recorded and released and films were being made, along with all the other activities that made up the John and Yoko show.

John told George Harrison that he needed help with the

renovations at Tittenhurst. George was very interested in all things Indian. He was learning to play the sitar and was friends with Ravi Shankar and other Indian musicians. He had become involved with the Hare Krishnas. They dressed in Indian clothes and sung chants to the Hindu God Krishna. Most of the Krishnas were Westerners and one saw them in public places, proselytising and begging for money. George suggested that in exchange for a place to stay, some of the Hare Krishnas could help with the renovations at Tittenhurst. John and Yoko agreed, and a group of about twenty of them turned up.

It was a time when a lot of young people were moving into all kinds of communes. There was something humorous about a group of middle-class Europeans dressed in traditional Indian clothes, devoting their lives to chanting Hindu prayers. Three times a day, they held services, or *kirtan,* in a large outbuilding on the property that was probably built as a squash court. In jest we called it the Temple. The Hare Krishnas were not very helpful at building. They did help Jill by looking after Sacha who, one day during *kirtan,* gave our dog Sam their shoes to play with. Whenever they went into *kirtan,* they left their shoes at the door of the Temple. Sam was a big black curly-haired bundle of energy and mischief. As the Krishnas sang, Sacha threw shoes for Sam, who carried them off into the undergrowth. By the end of *kirtan,* no one had a complete pair of shoes.

Most of my dealings were with a fellow named Eshan who was the most approachable. He was a young man who looked out of place in his Indian garb. I tried to get him and his cohorts to help us with the building, but they seemed to be unable to work for very long. They argued a lot among themselves about things that seemed trivial, like whose turn it was to take out the garbage.

The founder of the Hare Krishna movement, His Divine Grace A. C. Bhaktivedanta, also known as Swami Prabhupada, was drawn to John as if he was a magnet. On a visit, he moved in with his followers at Tittenhurst and wanted to meet John. The old man walked the grounds with one or two of the disciples, in a pale orange cotton dhoti with a shawl over his shoulders, wearing wellington boots.

A meeting was arranged with John and Yoko and, according to them, he proposed they make a deed of gift of all or part of Tittenhurst to the Hare Krishnas. John was not amused and Prabhupada left the next day.

John was definitely losing some of the Beatles' gullibility for holy men.

Living at Tittenhurst sometimes felt like being on the set of *The Wizard of Oz*. On one of the occasions when Yoko and John left their room, I took a walk with them and a fellow called Magic Alex. Alex was designing a sound recording studio for the basement of the Apple offices on Saville Row. Apparently he was saying that he could avoid the noise problems of central London by suspending the studio from the surrounding walls. No one quite seemed to understand how he would do this. Some of his projects had included an artificial sun, loudspeakers made of wallpaper, an invisible force-field around Ringo to get a clearer drum sound, and glowing paint that was supposed to make things disappear.

As we walked, he told John and Yoko that he had reason to believe they would be awarded the Nobel Peace Prize.

After the walk, John, who had become sceptical of Alex's promises, asked me to check him out. I took a trip into London to visit a workshop Alex had in a mews near Euston Station. It was a confused jumble of wire and electrical parts. I told John that I thought Alex's magic was only in the mind of the beholder.[4]

4 The recording studio that Alex Mardas built for the 'Let It Be' sessions had no soundproofing and no cables between the studio and the control room. According to Mark Lewisohn (in his book, *The Complete Beatles Chronicle*), 'the mixing console is made of bits of wood and an old oscilloscope and looked not unlike the control panel of a B-52 bomber'. Lewisohn also says

The days at Tittenhurst were taking on a semblance of normalcy as we moved into fall and work on the estate continued. I was fast becoming a buffer between John and Yoko and the sceptics at the Apple office.

Apple was suffering from a lack of any central control. If one of the Beatles had an idea, it would probably be adopted. Alex was just an extreme example of how gullible they could be. From the best intentions of establishing an environment for fostering young artists and creative ideas, Apple had become a chaotic entity, haemorrhaging money and spawning failures like the Apple Boutique. The accountants were trying to control expenses and they saw John and Yoko's projects as a continuation of the folly.

I was immersed in the numerous chores that needed to be done. Because of my antique stall on Portobello Road, I knew where to find antiques. One day I was at Harrods ordering white carpet to be specially made on extra large looms in China from natural unbleached wool. Another day, on a trip to town, I found white marble Empire mantle pieces. One of my favourite finds was a Queen Anne Chinoiserie desk for John. In their bathroom, they wanted a gigantic circular tub. We considered willow pattern antique toilets, but settled on modern ones. John wanted a bed like a phonograph turntable, so we ordered a circular bed.

An army of people was established to accomplish all these tasks. The builders were under the direction of a local contractor, gamely trying to keep up with changing plans and deadlines. Our own friends, who were also carpenters, did much of the speciality work. The housekeeper was Val Wilde a young energetic blonde girl who cooked and cleaned for John and Yoko. There always seemed to be drama in her life and much of it revolved around Andy, who

---

Alex was 'wandering around in a white coat, with a clipboard, muttering and trying to place box-loads of tiny loudspeakers around the studio, one for each track'. Alex was eventually fired by Allen Klein.

Dan Richter, a young actor in New York

Me in the mime play *The Godstuff* with the American Mime Theatre in 1962 at The Sharon Playhouse in Connecticut

Below
Paul J. Curtis and I in *The Scarecrow* at the American Mime Theatre

Erik Swartz and I in Izmir, Turkey, 1963 with a local boy on the way to India

Top right
Zina and Dan in our shikara – Srinagar in the spring of 1964

Below right
Me writing poetry and drawing on the deck of Zina Rachevsky's house boat *Soul Kiss* in Srinagar

Ron Vial, me and Peter Bendrey at the Shankaracharya temple high above Srinagar

Sacha Jung (left) and Ron Vial (right) in Srinagar in our shikara
Jed Curtis, at twenty-two, who introduced me to Yoko
Jill and I on our balcony in Athens with the first edition of our
poetry review *Residu* in the spring of 1965

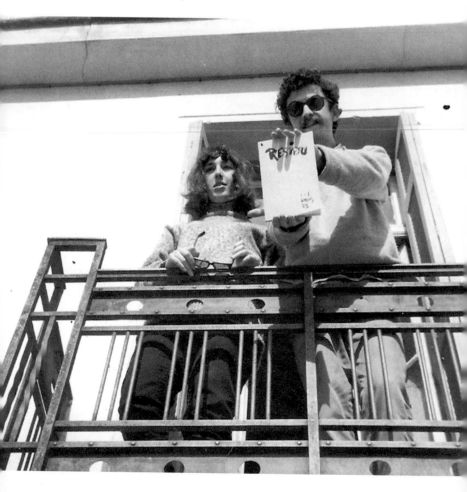

Jill and I in a photo booth in Athens

Jill and I at a poetry reading in London at the time of the Albert Hall Poetry Reading, 1965

Our wedding photo in front of the Kensington Registry Office with Jill wearing a Biba pant suit

The young choreographer and film star
Me as Moonwatcher in *2001: A Space Odyssey*

Tony Cox at Hanover Gate
Kyoko Cox at Hanover Gate

In recovery with Sacha

Off heroin, cleaned up, and ready to work again
with Jill and Sacha at Tittenhurst Park

Jill and Sacha with my mother Helen
in the garden at Tittenhurst Park

Mrs Thomas holding my beautiful
baby Mischa

John and Yoko in the garden just after we all moved into Tittenhurst Park.

John and Yoko through a doorway in Tittenhurst Park

John and Yoko during the *Fly* shoot
Yoko puts a fly on Virginia Lust during the shoot
Yoko holding a cup with flies in it

Top
I took this of John
and Yoko on stage
at the Toronto
Rock and Roll
Revival 1969

John and Yoko
meet Claudio, who
just wanted to look
in John's eyes, from
Imagine

Working on the
cover of the album
Imagine from the
film *Imagine*

Above John and Yoko and me with the attorney in Palma the night before
we 'kidnapped' Kyoko
Below Starting to look edgy again. In the limo from JFK to Manhattan
Facing Backstage in Madison Square Garden at the One to One Concert
Over Sacha and me at the Chelsea Hotel in New York. The dream was over

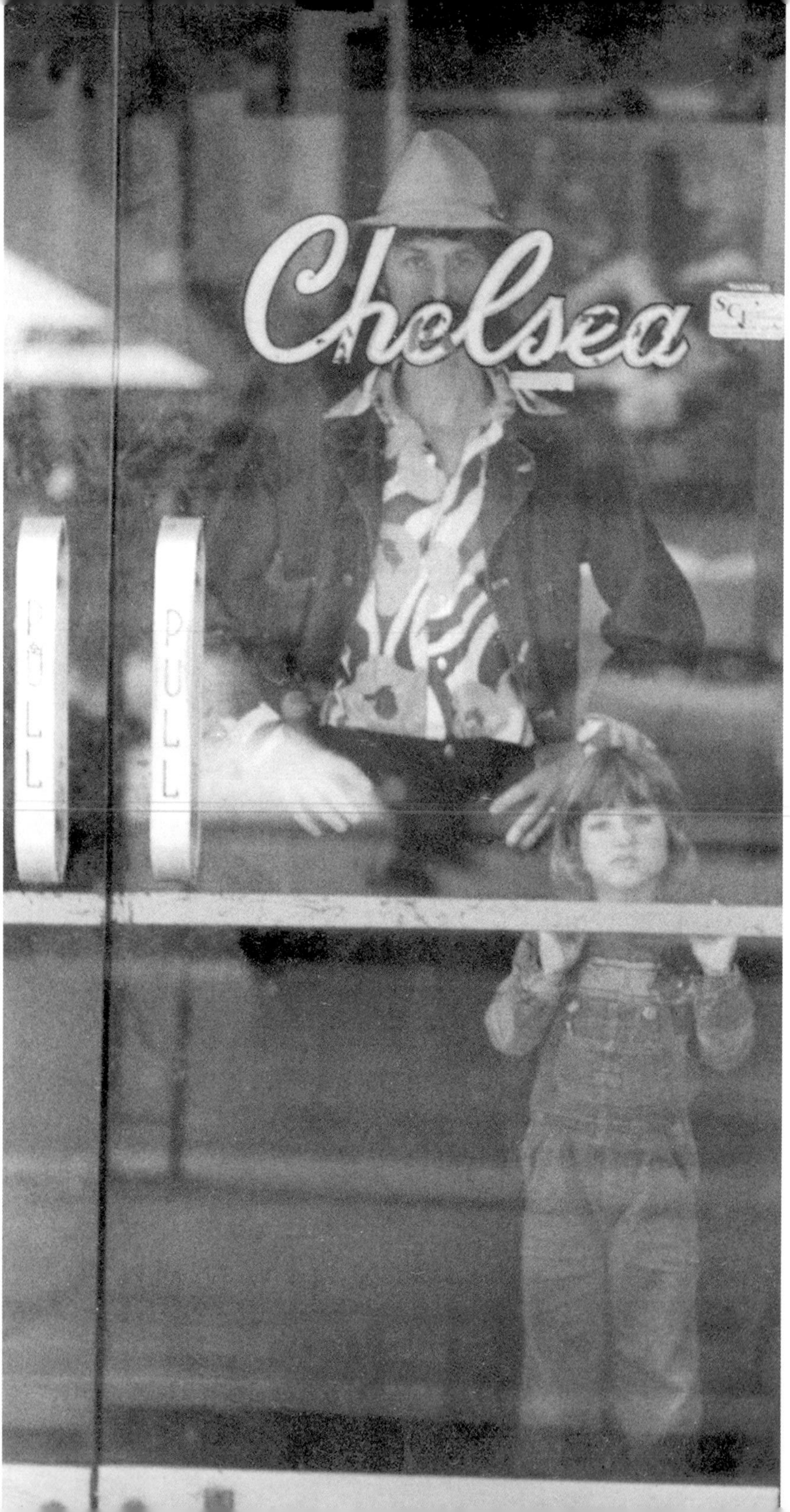
Chelsea
PULL
PULL

worked for Frank the gardener and drove around the grounds in a big white Land-Rover. We still had Les, the chauffeur who took John and Yoko into town in the long black Mercedes 600S limo they were using. Les was always mumbling and never content as he cared for the Mercedes and John's white Rolls.

John and Yoko wanted the office at Tittenhurst to fulfil many of the functions that were normally handled by the Apple office on Saville Row so Diana Robertson started coming down from London to do secretarial chores. Diana was good-looking, refreshingly sensible and luckily she had a sense of humour. Steven Brendell also arrived from Apple to do general assistant work. Steve was young and good-natured, and an aspiring drummer.

John bought golf carts for he and Yoko to use on their jaunts around the grounds. We also bought a bunch of wellington boots. The golf carts made it easier to get around the eighty-five acres of parkland at Tittenhurst, and the wellingtons were necessary since it rained a lot and the ground would be become wet and soggy.

John let me drive his little black Mini Cooper S.

'They made one for each of the Beatles,' he explained. They all had black velvet seats and enough sound equipment to constantly blow fuses. I had great fun sliding around corners on my way into Ascot to shop with some of the Hare Krishnas in the back seat, chanting in terror as I powered the little toy through each corner. John explained that he was never good with cars. He told me about a matt black Ferrari he bought that he used to go out to clubs. When he woke up in the morning, he would have no idea where he parked it; someone from Apple would have to go out and search for it. He had been driven around for a long time in a psychedelically-painted Rolls Royce that he eventually gave it to Allen Klien.

We had two donkeys that were too small for adults to ride, but perfect for Sacha. Of all the things at Ascot, he loved the donkeys best of all.

John and Yoko lived in bed. They spent most of their time there. They slept, ate, had sex, worked the phones, read the mail, planned their next outing, and whatever else that made up their day. During the morning, they summoned Val to bring them breakfast. Later, I would drop by to discuss what was going on or needed their attention. John was invariably sitting cross-legged on the bed strumming his acoustic guitar while Yoko took the lead in discussions. You always felt that Yoko and John had discussed things before you arrived and decided on what Yoko would say while John appeared to be lost in his guitar. He was listening, and whenever he chimed in, he always spoke with irony, humour, and directly to the point. John's keen intelligence and biting humour was a constant, just as was his idealism. He always had a unique take on everything. Even though he was heavily influenced by Yoko's agendas, everything he said came from him, unique, insightful, and humorous. He was always impatient and of course he and Yoko always wanted changes or something new for the building, which just prolonged the process. One morning, he told me that he wanted to wake up and be able to see water outside.

'Do you think we could put a lake out there?' John mused. I got the feeling he had been talking to George, who could see water from his windows.

'Why not? I'll look into it. I'll talk to the contractor,' I said.

They usually left the room for a walk so that Val could clean. Wearing great coats or army jackets, they ventured out onto the grounds to walk or ride about in one of the golf carts. I always found it intriguing that they were always in discussion. Their conversation was rich with ideas, projects, and causes. As isolated as John had to be to survive the enormous vortex of energy that surrounded him, he was completely in touch. They devoured newspapers, the trades, what limited TV England had to offer, bushels of mail, and the world through the telephones. Often Les drove them into town, or they were visited by a guest or someone from the office on an errand. There were always people coming down from London who were working on the various projects, like the cameraman and filmmaker Nic Knowland; the photographer Iain MacMillan, who had shot the *Abbey Road* cover; or the graphic designer, John Koch.

When guests arrived, they invariably sat at the big table in the kitchen and waited for John and Yoko who eventually came down from their room. Photographs and art work were laid out on the table where most of the work was done. After the meeting with John and Yoko, they drove back to London.

Sometimes Yoko and John came out of their room bursting with a new idea. One day they planned a great party or event where they were going to have a guest list that includes Liz Taylor, Richard Burton, and the Pope. It didn't come to pass, but the excitement they generated about it was real.

All around them was this great unfinished mansion. Some of the rooms were temporarily set up for their use, others were filled with workmen on scaffolds scraping and painting, everywhere walls were being demolished or built. Empty rooms were filled with the flotsam and jetsam of the Beatles phenomenon. Boxes were stacked everywhere, filled with colourful clothing and costumes, shoes and boots, books, acetates, records, hundreds of tapes, guitars, baubles, and enumerable gifts.

I often sorted through the boxes in an attempt to make some sense of it all. I was collecting all the tapes and records for the archives. Jill and I were looking through the boxes one afternoon when we found an old framed antique flyer for a show that John said was his source and inspiration for *Sergeant Pepper's Lonely Hearts Club Band.* Upstairs, John was moving forward, leaving the great Beatles juggernaut behind him. I wondered if he thought he would ever be able to get free from it. Meanwhile the fighting with Paul was intensifying.

John's career as an artist was progressing. The second show of his own art work opened January 16, 1970 with an exhibition of lithographs called *Bag One* at the London Arts Gallery. Some of the lithographs were erotic drawings of him and Yoko having sex. It was a limited edition of 300 sets and each set contained 14 lithographs hand-signed by John. Each set was put in a large white portfolio briefcase. They were line drawings in the simple doodle-like style that he and Yoko had developed. They both had always drawn in the same sparse way. Even before they met, John's book of poetry, *A Spaniard in the Works,* and Yoko's book of instructions, *Grapefruit,* were both very similar. Both had simple line drawings and John's had story-poems while Yoko's had terse, often poetic, instructions. The longer they were together, the more their drawing seems to meld so that looking at one it was often hard to tell which one of them drew it.

The lithographs were very sexy, naïve, delightful, and had created quite a stir. The London police confiscated eight of them in a raid. An important part of their art was the reaction it produced. As Yoko became more famous because of her relationship with John, her own art seemed to lose some of its austerity and much of the ambiguity and mystery that had been part of her image. Perhaps her own credibility as an artist was being somehow compromised. While they presented themselves as equal partners, they were often perceived as John with Yoko riding along on his coat tails.

While all this was going on, I was surreptitiously taking a mini cab into London to buy heroin. I took the cab instead of the Mini Cooper so that Les wouldn't know. Through Alex Trocchi, I had met an old junkie named Janet who could still get heroin legally. Up until two years before, addicts could get prescriptions for heroin. Then the policy changed and addicts were moved onto Methadone. A few older longtime addicts like Janet were allowed to stay on heroin. Somehow, Janet had survived and she would sell me some of her large daily prescription. I used to take a cab from Ascot to her bed-sit in North London. The cab waited outside while I went in to see her. She sat in her bed in the corner of her little room; a grimy curtain covered her only window. She looked like an ancient rumpled bird. She didn't even bother to lift her night gown when she gave herself a shot. Her veins had been ruined so she just stuck the needle in her thigh right through it. Poor Janet's voice was more of a croak than speech. As I watched her I wondered if that would be me one day. I gave her the cash and she gave me the heroin pills. Then the cab took me back to Ascot.

On returning to Tittenhurst, I would lock myself in my bathroom, take out a clean syringe and inject myself with enough of the drug to take the nagging sickness away. If I had enough, I might even get a bit high. Once I was comfortable, I would go up to John and Yoko's area and quietly put some outside their bedroom door then called Yoko and let her know it was there. Unlike grass and cocaine, we never used the heroin together.

Cold Turkey

In my heart I will always be six years old. I have a black and white photograph of me at my sixth birthday party. It is a beautiful June day and I am on the lawn at our family house in Darien, Connecticut. It is a comfortable and secure environment cushioned by money. I am wearing a shorts suit from Best and Company and little shoes that attach with buckles. I am surrounded by my friends Bonnie Brooks, Fluffy Crimins, Cynthia Gile and all my other schoolmates. The little girls are wearing party pinafores. The year is 1945, The Second World War is ending and there is happiness and promise in the air. I will never be so happy and secure again.

Kicking heroin forces the junkie to change and evolve. The emotional problems of addiction have to be dealt with, but he also gets very sick when he stops. Junkies experiences extreme agitation, cramps, and all kinds of aches and pains. They are either soaked with sweat or shuddering with cold. Other drugs are given to help the symptoms of withdrawal; they sedate him but he still can't sleep. Most of the physical symptoms pass in a few days leaving him emotionally naked. All the feelings and fears that he was burying with the heroin now have to be confronted. This is the hardest part and can only be endured if the junkie is willing to grow and change.

As the winter of 1970 approached, John and Yoko decided to stop using heroin before they became more seriously addicted. I was scared because I was so entrenched in my long-term addiction and I had never succeeded in quitting. With the screwed-up logic of a junkie, I resented them as 'chippies', the term we used for people who dabbled in the drug. Actually, John had gone through prolonged battles with addiction and alcoholism for years.

110

Once John and Yoko stopped using, I become a problem for them. I knew John wanted me to leave. I felt that unless I quit too, Jill, Sacha and I would have to go. I dreaded another attempt at a cure and feared another failure. I had fought addiction for four years. What began as an imprudent experiment in consciousness expansion had turned into an uncontrollable nightmare. I never meant to become an addict.

Realising that I had to do something, I met with John and Yoko in their bedroom to discuss the problem. The conversation went something like this.

'Dan, we can't have you around knowing you are using heroin. It would drive us crazy knowing it was here. We couldn't stand the temptation,' said John, looking right at me.

'I know, John, I want to kick so badly, but it's not that easy, I've been fighting this for four years now. I'm afraid of another failure,' I said.

'If you're afraid, you can't achieve anything,' he said. He paused and then looking right at me he asked, 'What do you need to be able to kick?'

I sensed that he really wanted to give me the chance to end it. I thought hard for a few moments and said, 'I'd need total isolation for a long time. I'd need a doctor on call to get me through the first week of withdrawal and then help me stabilise on methadone until I can trust myself around people again.'

There was a silence for a moment and he and Yoko looked at each other. Then John said, 'Well, you can do that here.'

Yoko and John arranged everything. Every day we were to give Val a shopping list and she would order everything we needed. They asked Mike Loxton, a local doctor, to come and check me daily and supply medication to get me through the mental and physical agony of the first weeks. Then he would help me stabilise on Methadone. John and Yoko made sure that everything was taken care of so I could stay secluded during the cure.

As the treatment progressed, even with Methadone to help, I rolled about in my sweat-soaked sheets. Delirium, dreams, and memories filled my head. I relived all the agonies of past cures.

Two weeks passed and I did not use heroin. The nights were strange and dreamlike. Kicking horse spaced me out. I was in a cold, clear dream, no warmth, no comfort. I could only manage fitful periods of sleep. I was so tired and I was not tired. I knew that each night would be long and without the respite of sleep, or the oblivion of heroin. I was gripped in a vice of cold despair.

I could see Jill sleeping beside me, her face washed by the cold moonlight. In the other room, Sacha slept soundly. I couldn't stop worrying about him. Maybe he had stopped breathing? 'Damn it, Dan,' I said to myself. 'You've been lying here for over an hour. Get up and take a look.' As I padded in, I saw that, like Jill, he was lit by the moon's light coming through his window. He was making little snuffing sounds as if the moon was making him dream. He was just fine. I bent over his crib, and as I kissed him, I could smell the warm baby smell, a mixture of sweat, milk, powder, and diapers.

One night I looked out of the window and saw the donkey field illuminated by the cold moon. The shakes, sweats, and chills were over. I had made it that far. I swore to myself, 'This time I am really going to do it. No one ever died from lack of sleep.'

John and Yoko were away a lot, visiting Toronto for the Peace Festival and spending time at a farm in Denmark where Tony and Kyoko were living. The energy level dropped and Ascot took on an eerie quiet when they weren't there. This was good for me while I was coming off heroin. It gave me the time I needed to deal with my feelings and the physical pain of withdrawal. A calm settled over me about two weeks after my initial withdrawal. It was a fragile calmness and I felt that if the smallest thing happened, like somebody talking to me, it would shatter and I would have to use drugs to get my balance and sanity back. I felt as if I was in a delicate foggy bubble moving through space and if the bubble chanced to bump against something or someone it would burst and I would no longer be protected. Each morning after I got up and had my breakfast I slid my feet into my Wellington boots and went out walking the grounds. Tittenhurst Park and the surrounding land covers many acres. From the main house the lawns slope down in a gentle arc past a statue of Diana the Huntress and the lake to the woods and fields below. I estimated that at least a third of the grounds were planted with exotic trees and banks of rhododendron and azalea. The trees and shrubs must have been planted when the park was laid out in 1769. Once it had been open to the public. There were little bronze plaques stuck in the ground beside each of the trees showing their common and Latin names. Some of the Weeping Blue Atlas Cedars and willows were so large that their overhanging branches touched the ground. All I had to do was push through into their peaceful centres where I sat quietly on the beds of leaves that had fallen there. These spots were peaceful little rooms, refuges where light filtered through the leaves that formed them. It was absolutely magical.

In these sanctuaries I would think about what had happened to my life. Often my thoughts were dominated by the memories of David. I would go over and over in my mind to see if there was anything I could have done to change what happened. With a nagging sense of guilt I knew if I hadn't been an addict, things would have been different. When you first come off heroin you feel like a piece of crystal shattered into thousands of pieces. You try to put all those pieces back together but the job is insurmountable. The pieces never seem to fit and the edges are often sharp and cut you. You have to learn acceptance and patience. Your dopamine receptors are screwed up and change how you deal with every little detail of your life. Your ears are so fragile that even the smallest sound can be intensely irritating. In my quiet cocoon I could sit for hours on end allowing all the little pieces to slowly find their way back together again. My body was mending too. The wounds and sores left by the syringe needle were slowly healing. Dr Loxton gave me antibiotics and antiseptic creams and the tracks on my arms were turning into scars.

As the weeks passed I felt stronger both physically and mentally. I began to walk to the outer reaches of the park. As I picked my way among the vast rhododendron hedges, I discovered wooden fences with fields beyond. Most of these fields had gone to seed. In one were the two donkeys John and Yoko had bought. They spent their days methodically munching on grass and gave me querulous looks whenever I walked by them. Out beyond the donkey field was a little copse of trees. The undergrowth around it had been allowed to grow wild and walking there I felt as though I was touching the natural order of things. I was taken back to my youth in Connecticut when I used to cross the lawn in our backyard and journey into our woods. When I was seven or eight, being alone in nature made me feel safe and complete. I developed a love of wild places untouched by human hand.

As a recovering addict and alcoholic, I look back at myself then with a profound sadness. There was a futility to my efforts. I believed that the Methadone Dr Loxton was giving me was a cure. It allowed me to stop using needles, to stop the endless roller coaster ride of injection, rush, and a brief high followed by a debilitating sickness that could only be cured by another shot. The addict has a hubris that allows him to believe he is on a path to success. We call it denial. It is a defining symptom of the disease we have. I look back at myself as I was then, sitting in the wombs of those willow trees, wracked with guilt and calmed by the methadone and marijuana that I was still smoking, believing my terrible journey was ending when indeed it was only just beginning.

As heroin began to fade into the background, John and Yoko's political involvements became less peaceful. In January of 1970 they cut off all their hair and auctioned it to raise money for Michael X's Black House in Islington. The Black House was a complex of adjoining terrace houses, shops, and empty factories in the Holloway Road. Michael, now leader of the Black Muslims in England, was converting the properties into a black commune with the help of volunteers.

John and Yoko had read *The Primal Scream* by the psychiatrist Dr Arthur Janov. He wrote about getting in touch with the primal self, the child within, and releasing all the pent-up pain and anger buried during childhood. Yoko and John invited him to come to Ascot in March of 1970 so they could take his treatment. He treated them in the unfinished sound studio. Since his treatment involved going back to experience early feelings and then letting everything out in a primal scream, it was an excellent site for his work. The walls were already insulated for sound so they could scream as loud as they wanted and no one would hear them. They were totally into it and Ascot became for a time a private psychiatric hospital. John had a lot of buried pain and anger that Janov brought out in the muted seclusion of the raw studio space.

I noticed how John and Yoko shifted from one intense experience to the next. They were one hundred percent committed to whatever cause they were involved in.

One spring day I followed Val with the breakfast tray up to John and Yoko's bedroom. They were in bed.

'Stanley Kubrick has contacted me. He heard that the editing table is finally being shipped and wants to borrow it.' I said.

With the help of film technicians, I had designed a film editing machine for them. It was a table with three screens, able to run both sixteen and thirty-five millimeter films, and handle all kinds of sound. Prevost in Italy had been building it since the fall and it was just about ready.

'Wow, Stanley Kubrick – that's really cool. We're off to LA with Art Janov; we won't be able to use it till we come back. Tell him

Yoko and I would be happy to lend it to him.' John looked impressed.

'Yes, that would be cool,' Yoko agreed.

A few days later I met with Stanley at his home, Abbott's Mead, just North of London. He was wearing a crumpled blue suit jacket and his beard was short and stubbly. It was one of those perfect English spring days. I had left the security of Ascot to supervise the installation of John and Yoko's editing table in Stanley's garage. We hadn't seen each other for over a year. I was still shaky from my cure but it felt great to be out.

'Dan, I can make any picture with eight people right here at home.' Stanley talked enthusiastically as we walked from his house to his garage where he was editing his latest movie, *A Clockwork Orange*.

'How didya get together with John Lennon?' he asked in his Bronx accent.

'I met him through Yoko Ono. She's an old friend.'

'I heard they are making pictures,' he said.

'Yeah, experimental stuff. Yoko made films as part of her conceptual art work and now she and John are working on them together. She made a film called *Bottoms* or *Film Number 4* that got a lot of publicity. It repeated the same shot of different people's bottoms while they walked on a treadmill. The sound track was the voices of the people talking as they were being filmed.'

Inside Stanley's garage, technicians were setting up the Prevost editing table. There was a small Steenbeck flatbed editing table already in use. Off in a corner was Stanley's traditional stand-up Moviola editor.

Stanley sat down at the Steenbeck and showed me some of the footage from *A Clockwork Orange*. There were scenes set in a vivid crisp future with Malcolm McDowell playing Alex, a young psychopath.

'That's great footage Stanley,' I said. 'It's so different from *2001*.'

'Well, they're both set in the future,' he said with a smile.

'How can you make a picture in your garage when you need sets, equipment, and people?' I asked.

'No problem,' Stanley replied. 'If we need to work on a larger set, we just have it built at a studio and go there, shoot, and then come back here. I have all the space I need right here for our offices and editing. Come on, I'll show you.'

In his office back up at the house, we examined his IBM Selectric typewriters and the Telex machine.

'With the Telex I can get sales figures from Hollywood minutes after they have them,' he said proudly. 'And look at this shredder, it has very strong blades and cuts the paper twice so it can't be put back together.'

'Man that's great. I've got to get one for Tittenhurst; the one I have now is pretty flimsy.'

Meanwhile on April 10, 1970 Paul McCartney told the press that he was quitting the Beatles and two weeks later on the 23rd John and Yoko left for LA.

A peacefulness descended on Tittenhurst with Yoko and John gone. The frenetic activity that surrounded them had followed them to LA and I found myself back in the quiet safe environment where I could work on my recovery. Val continued to bring us supplies and true to my regimen I rarely left the property. The world was safely at bay on the other side of the walls of the estate. I was a self-exiled prisoner in a dendrologist's paradise.

Outside my refuge the world was in turmoil. On May 4th at Kent State University in Ohio, four students were shot and killed while protesting a massive American-South Vietnamese troop offensive into Cambodia that Nixon had just announced. 'They're starting to kill us,' I thought.

With the return of my health, I began to catalogue John and Yoko's collection of tapes and films. I also involved myself full time with the design and building of the new facilities.

Both the house and I were being refurbished together. In this process, bit by bit, I became the unpaid chamberlain of the facilities and the activities that took place there.

As my recovery from heroin progressed, it was good for me to have all this work to do. With John and Yoko away, we were really close to completing the work of rebuilding. At the bottom of the garden, after a hold-up to remove an unexploded World War II bomb, John's new lake was just about completed. It was a tough but good time for me, full of pain, hope, and rebirth.

Although I had stopped daily use of heroin, I had traded it for Methadone maintenance. Booze was used in extreme moderation especially after John returned. He could be a violent drunk. We both had used drugs in lieu of drinking as we had serious problems with alcohol in the past.

A Working Class Hero

The warm, lush English summer of 1970 was ending and life was really starting to look a lot better for me. Thanks to John and Yoko giving me a refuge in which to kick heroin, my health was returning. I was stabilised on a moderate daily dose of the Methadone prescribed by Dr Loxton and trying to use marijuana and hashish in moderation. I tried to avoid alcohol. As a teenager I had abused it and I was a bad drunk. It made me uncomfortable, so when people were drinking, I would drink Coca-Cola with a slice of lemon. Occasionally I would drink a glass of wine at a dinner party.

The work of renovating the house and installing recording and filming facilities was beginning to pay off. The studio took longer but the editing room and colour darkroom were operational. John and Yoko returned from Los Angeles and the Janov therapy. They had stayed with him in treatment until John's immigration problems forced them back to Ascot. They seemed refreshed and had a new vitality. The US had affected them. John loved the energy and the people. For him, America was the centre of the world and rock and roll was its music. He loved being a king in the land of rock and roll. One day he asked me, 'Who do you think is bigger, me or Elvis?'

Apparently a kind of self-indulgence was part of or a result of Janov's treatment, and at John's request, we filled the big new freezer with all kinds of ice cream. John had also developed a taste for Dr Pepper that was sent over from the States by the case.

Every day we sat around the large kitchen table drinking tea and eating ice cream while we dealt with daily business. Letters were opened, communications from the Apple office read, plans made and letters dictated to Diana.

John was writing music. He either had a guitar in his hand or was tinkling on a piano. Using the deeply personal material he gleaned from the primal therapy, he created what he called the *Plastic Ono Band* album. Yoko was working on a matching album, which included recordings of the Albert Hall concert with Ornette. Since the studio at Ascot was not ready, all the Plastic Ono Band material was recorded at Abbey Road.

One day Yoko, remembering the photographic work I did at Hanover Gate said, 'Dan, why don't you photograph us for the cover of our albums?'

I was very excited – what a great opportunity, I was going to do a cover of a John Lennon album.

John showed me an idyllic line drawing he had done of a man sitting with his back against a tree, holding a woman in his arms. They wanted identical covers based on the drawing, with John's cover a picture of Yoko holding him and Yoko's the reverse.

We went out into the grounds to find the perfect tree. John had so much fun going from tree to tree. He reminded me of a puppy, romping around Yoko as we searched. He had the drawing in his hand and examined each tree for the perfect look.

I wanted to create a dreamy soft effect to go with the mood of the drawing so, rather than use my Nikon, I decided to use the cheapest plastic camera I could find with a lens that wouldn't be crisp. I developed the pictures in our new darkroom and pushed the negative until the colours began to break up. This produced a Seurat-like pointillist effect. In discussion with John and Yoko, it was decided to use baby pictures of each of them for the reverse side of each album. I enlarged the photos for the back covers of each album. John's picture broke up into the points of its printed source, which added to the overall effect. With the design elements complete, John Kosh, the graphic designer who was working at Apple, put them all together. Aside from the recording at Abbey Road, all the work on the albums was done at Tittenhurst Park.

What's wrong with a Working Class Hero?

JOHN LENNON / PLASTIC ONO BAND

YOKO ONO / PLASTIC ONO BAND

Apple Records

All compositions published by Maclen (Music) Ltd, 3 Savile Row, W1

We were on our way to creating a one-stop shop and I was part of the creative input.

The sales of John's album were small and Yoko's smaller. The Apple office, not seeing a Beatles hit album, was deeply critical, particularly of Yoko. Accustomed to the massive sales associated with a Beatle record, they were blind to what John and Yoko were trying to do. They saw these albums as evidence of how Yoko's influence was destroying John and breaking up the Beatles. Most people didn't understand that John did not want to be limited to making more 'Beatle' music. He was moving on and needed the freedom to experiment with new forms. Few people understood that Yoko was a trained musician and for the most part she was not trying to sing in a traditional rock and roll style. She was trained in Japanese singing forms that might sound strange to Western ears. They were both accomplished musicians producing ground-breaking and exciting work.

John and Yoko, while hurt by the criticism, remained unfazed; the next album, *Imagine*, would be produced entirely at Tittenhurst.

I was aware of John's pain as he was exposed to all this. When I passed on the British sales figures from Apple for both albums, I sensed John's conflict at knowing how few sold compared to Beatles albums. It took a lot of courage to resist the pressure put on him.

The house was starting to look really good. The completed areas had a cool, minimalist elegance. In the great white room off the main entrance hall, Yoko had placed some of her best art pieces including her all white chessboard with all white chess pieces. Climbing the white-carpeted main stairs one passed an array of her hammer and nail pieces. These consisted of a wood panel with a hammer hanging from it on a chain. Nails were provided which viewers were encouraged to hammer in. On the wall beside the stripped wood door to their bedroom hung a collection of antique Japanese masks.

Fly and *Up Your Legs Forever*

It was the first week of December 1970 and John, Yoko and I were going to New York for the release of their Plastic Ono Band albums. It was my first time back in the States for a year and a half and also the first time I had travelled with them as a business associate. My position had changed since their return from Bel Air and the completion of the *Plastic Ono Band* albums. Free from heroin and rehabilitated, I was working with them full time. I had become a jack of all trades doing everything from photographing record covers, editing film, archiving tapes, running their affairs, and riding shotgun for just about everything they did. For my new self it was exhilarating. I liked being so busy, it made staying off heroin that much easier. I didn't care that I was working on someone else's projects instead of my own. When I wasn't working with them, fuelled by my new heroin-free energy, I was creating some of the best paintings and poetry I had ever done. I was swept up in being involved with the greatest Rock star of all time.

Armed with mixes and acetates, I had arrived in New York before John and Yoko. I was very nervous travelling to New York. Aside from my trip to see Stanley Kubrick and a few visits to the Apple office, this was my first time out since my cure and I was still gun shy. I brought my Methadone with me and even though it was on a legal prescription from Dr Loxton, I imagined big problems if the customs or police found it. I could just see me saying in a trembling voice, 'Yes, officer, I am a legal drug addict.'

Flying first class on the new Pan AM 747 was very cool. There was great food, pleasant stewardesses, and an upper deck with a lounge and a bar at the top of a spiral staircase. I settled my nerves by surreptitiously eating a bit of Afghani hash and drinking rum and cokes at the bar. I had a very mellow trip as we flew into the setting sun.

When I stepped onto the tarmac at JFK it was very cold and icy. The wind was blowing so I raised my velvet collar and grabbed my hat. As I walked toward the terminal, a stocky man in a loud jacket and a customs officer pulled me out of the group. 'Oh shit, I'm busted,' I thought. The stocky man asked me if I was Dan Richter.

'Y–yes.'

'Great, I was afraid I wouldn't recognise you. I'm Pete Bennett. I work with Allen, Allen Klein. I do the record promotion for Allen's clients. This guy will check you out.'

I showed my passport and declaration card to the customs officer who OK'd me and walked away.

'We have friends at the airport,' Pete said, with a smile, as he helped me into a waiting limo.

'8-track sounds great, huh?' said Pete as stereo sound filled the vehicle. Outside in the night, the lights of Queens slid by. While I had been back in the States for our short stay in Provincetown, I hadn't been in New York for over six years. The city seemed dirtier than Europe, chaotic, somehow dangerous. I left New York in black and white and mono and I was returning in colour and stereo. 'The office got you a loan of a private apartment on Central Park South. I think it belongs to some writer dame, Jacqueline Susanne or somebody like that. This stereo FM is cool, huh?'

'I'll be home for Christmas, darling.' Jill sounded so far away.

'No, I'm not in a hotel. ABKO, Allen Klein's company, put me in an apartment. It looks like something out of the *Valley of the Dolls*, white, pink, and puffy.'

Allen's office occupied most of the northwest corner of the 41st floor at Broadway and 53rd Street. He was very proud of the Italian woodwork he had commissioned. As he looked me over, he described the Italian workmen who had installed it and the exorbitant sum of money he spent on it. Allen was stocky, of medium height, with short curly hair. As he talked, I could see the orphan boy from New Jersey who with hard work and a gift for mental maths had scrambled to the top of the music business.

'You can use this office.' Paul Mozian was one of Allen's assistants. He was young and bright with a savvy Bronx accent. He helped me settle in and introduced me to everyone. Allan Steckler was a friendly, knowledgeable fellow who did the A & R work. May Pang was there, too. May was working as an assistant. She was wonderfully cheery and energetic, with a disarmingly delightful New York accent.

A few days later, John and Yoko arrived and we moved into the Plaza. As soon as they were settled we went over to Allen's office to discuss Yoko's desire to make two films. Each script was a short paragraph from her book *Grapefruit*. Allen's idea for a film was something more like *A Hard Day's Night* or *Help*. Yoko and John had been exploring conceptual forms since they got together. They intended to continue working in the experimental and conceptual vein they had begun with their short films *Two Virgins* and *Smile*. Both of these films were made with fixed slow motion cameras dissolving between images of Yoko and John. Yoko had some success and notoriety with *Film Number 4* or *Bottoms*. This film had brought her to the attention of the public in London and was the high point of her career at that time.

'Dan can help,' Yoko explained to Allen. 'He did the Albert Hall poetry reading and helped me with my concert with Ornette Coleman. And he starred in Stanley Kubrick's 2001: A Space Odyssey and choreographed it, too.'

Allen gave me a dirty look as I nodded to assure him that it was all quite possible.

Poor Allen – only the year before he had won John over and become the Beatles manager. Now he had an obligation to keep on John's good side, but he obviously saw the films as pure madness that would ultimately damage the value of the Beatles brand. He argued that he could get them a great film deal with a 'real' film company or studio. To make two films like these was not in their best interests. John and Yoko wouldn't be swayed. Allen soon realised that they were going to do exactly what they wanted.

The next order of business was René Magritte. John had expressed an interest in the paintings of this delightful surrealist. Allen had found a dealer with a Magritte for sale and he was waiting to show them the painting. In walked the dealer with a Magritte, floating umbrellas, bowler hats, and all.

'Johnny!'

To my surprise, my buddy from the Albert Hall days, John Esam, was helping the dealer carry in the painting.

'Danny, how are you?'

Everyone was a bit nonplussed by our exuberance. The painting was beautiful, and as Johnny and I caught up, John and Yoko examined it. They took a rain check on the picture and we left to go down to the Village to visit with Jonas Mekas at the Anthology Film Archives.

Jonas Mekas was an independent filmmaker. He was a nervously intelligent and wiry man devoted to independent films. He created the Anthology Film Archives, a repository for an extensive collection of independent, underground, and experimental films. Jonas was very interested in the films that John and Yoko were making and wanted to put on a John and Yoko film festival at New York's Elgin Theatre in about two weeks time. John and Yoko decided that Yoko would make the two films based on her book *Grapefruit* for the Elgin screenings. They would be called *Up your Legs Forever* and *Fly*. We set out to make the films in less than two weeks. I was tasked with organising the productions and the first order of business was to get local crews and filmmakers to help.

'This is Steve Gebhardt,' Jonas said as a tall, blond, moustached Middle Westerner came out of the projection booth at the Archives.

Steve was a conceptual filmmaker and big fan of Yoko's work. In Steve and his partner Bob Fries, Jonas had found the perfect people for John and Yoko to work with. Steve and Bob were from the Cincinnati 'underground film mafia.' Bob had a small production company, Robert Fries Films. Bob was a curly-haired urbane film and music guy with all kinds of equipment and recording expertise. Both he and Steve were rock fans as well as knowing about Yoko's work. They saw no difficulty in shooting two films in less than two weeks and we set about getting the productions underway. I turned part of Allen's ABKO offices into an ad hoc production office. Allen's assistants Paul Mozian and May Pang were seconded to help. Paul had a down-to-earth New Yorker's savvy and May, the consummate fan, was excited to work with John and Yoko.

The first film we shot was *Up Your Legs Forever.* The script called for the camera to track from a person's feet up their legs, then restart at the next set of feet. Yoko conceived it as a repetitive film in the manner of her *Film Number 4. Up Your Legs* followed the same idea of using the same shot over and over. Yoko decided to make the sound track the same way as in *Film Number 4.* We would record the conversations taking place between the participants, filmmakers, and crew as they prepared, watched, and took part in the picture.

With all the elements decided on by Yoko, Steve, Bob, and I set about getting it all together. We needed a stage, a dolly, a camera, recording equipment, and a lot of bathrobes. The bathrobes were for the participants to wear before and after they did their part. And, of course, we needed people. This was going to be a blast!

The second film, *Fly,* called for a fly to come through an open window into a room where a naked woman was lying on a bed. The fly was to land on the woman's body, walk around on it, and then fly back out the window. Yoko wanted to follow the fly with an extreme close-up lens so that the contours and shapes of the woman's body would become a fleshy landscape. She and John would create the sound track. We needed a naked woman, a lot of flies, a bed, a camera with a close-up lens, some lights, and a place to shoot it. This was going to be a lot easier than *Up your Legs* and, with a naked woman, a lot more fun.

Bob and Steve found us a studio up by Columbus Circle. As we started to shoot *Up your Legs,* John and Yoko sat on director's chairs behind Steve who was mounted on a mechanised camera dolly in front of a white cyclorama. We wanted to shoot three hundred and sixty-five people so there was an endless stream coming in to be photographed. Through celebrity friends like Andy Warhol, the word went out for volunteers and a who's who of the rock and art worlds showed up to take off their pants and have their legs filmed.

Through Steve, and Bob, scores of people from the downtown art scene turned up; Warhol superstar wannabes, artists, hangers-on, the famous, and the almost famous. Paul and May collected a colourful cross section of music business people of every kind. Everyone to be photographed was ushered into a dressing room to remove their clothing from the waist down and put on a terry cloth bathrobe. As they came out, Yoko instructed them to stand on the marks in front of the camera.

I then adjusted them and said, 'May I take your robe?'

John watched, sometimes strumming his guitar, and sometimes making a helpful or humorous comment or pun.

The camera started at their feet and tracked up their legs to their bottoms. The idea was to dissolve them all together to make an endless stream of legs with the illusion of the camera steadily rising.

For the sound track, we placed Nagra tape recorders around the stage and dressing room area to record the conversations of those who had come to be filmed or to watch. These would be edited and cut together to form the sound track of the movie.

John and Yoko were in their element. Yoko was making two films with the world watching her and John was sitting right in the middle of the art world. They were the major focus of all that was hip and happening in New York. Everyone wanted to see them, talk to them, or just be around them. Hundreds of people were taking their pants off in public. Yoko once again, as in *Film Number 4*, had persuaded people to be naked before the world.

Back at the ABKO office, John was interviewed by January Wenner for *Rolling Stone*. January looked like a high school kid or a fan. He brought with him the young Annie Leibovitz to photograph John for the cover.

'Steve, move in closer.' Yoko leant over Steve Gebhardt who was down between the legs of the underground actress Virginia Lust. Steve was shooting a drugged fly that was staggering around Virginia's vagina. It was only a few days later and we were already filming the second film, *Fly*. We were ensconced in the Bowery loft of the photographer and filmmaker Robert Frank. Robert shared the loft with our friend, underground filmmaker Danny Seymour. For almost twenty-four hours, Steve and Bob were shooting, with a close-up lens, drugged flies that were staggering around Virginia Lust's naked body as Yoko directed over their shoulders. Virginia's body becomes a landscape from the hills of her breasts to the dark valley of her vagina.

'If I get any closer, I'll get my ears wet,' said Steve, who was getting frustrated. We were shooting around the clock and we were very tired. Yoko was tireless.

Casting was our first problem. I was surprised how many women were prepared to lie naked on their backs with their legs spread open as flies walked all over every part of their bodies. We auditioned a lot of women, but most of them could not stay motionless. Virginia Lust, who was a participant in *Up You Legs Forever*, was able to lie completely still without flinching when the fly was put on her. A little heroin appeared to help and Virginia even managed to nod off. I was still clean so I avoided getting involved. I didn't need that kind of temptation.

The next and biggest problem was how to get a fly to walk

around on Virginia's body and not fly away. I had learned how to drug a fly during the shooting of *2001: A Space Odyssey*. You take a paper cup, put a fly in it, and put a plastic cover on it. You then blow carbon dioxide through the drinking hole in the plastic cover and the fly passes out. If you don't give it too much CO_2, the fly will wake up and walk around for a minute before it flies away. If the fly has too much, it may wobble for a second and then die, rolling over with its little feet in the air.

While we were getting the CO_2, someone found us a supply of flies apparently from South America. When they arrived, they were all dead. We began a frantic search for flies and enlisted anyone who would help by going around to restaurant kitchens. We paid by the fly.

'I'll never eat in Horn & Hardart[5] again,' muttered Bob. Some people came back with Horn & Hardart paper coffee cups with lots of flies in them.

We finally finished the shoot and with *Fly* in the can, John and Yoko edited it in one night in a suite at the Regency with Danny Seymour. Danny was a heroin addict, so I steered clear of him as well.

The Elgin was an old theatre in Chelsea. We scrambled to get everything ready for the showings. We only had five days left so we were working around the clock. Since there was no time to make composite prints, we brought in double-system projectors that could show the print and play the sound track in sync. The films were shown to a sold-out crowd. *Up your Legs* didn't work as well as *Film Number 4* had. It seemed long and the illusion of endless legs didn't work. Each shot didn't flow into the next as Yoko hoped it would. *Fly* on the other hand was well accepted. The gigantic fly moving around the body landscape worked. It was too

5 Horn & Hardart was the ubiquitous Automat you used to see in New York.

long, though. We cut it down to a shorter version and showed it in the spring at Cannes.

As the year ended, Paul McCartney began High Court proceedings to end the Beatles partnership. John said it was Paul's fault that the Beatles had broken up.

'It's because he wanted to dominate us all,' he said

It would be cool to go to Cannes.

Power to the People

Back at Ascot, during the early spring of 1971, things were in full swing. Most of the renovations were complete. The kitchen was now a beautiful large space with stainless steel appliances and counters. In the middle of the quarry tile floor, stood a great monastery table that could seat over a score of people. The kitchen could now be accessed directly from the editing and screening rooms above by a Victorian wrought iron spiral staircase. There was always someone new sitting around the table. One day it was Ernie Eban with a crew from Japanese TV waiting to interview Yoko. Another time it was Dick Gregory eager to discuss all the great uses for human urine which included using it for shampoo and drinking it.

Yoko sometimes revealed her dark side. Late one afternoon we were talking in the editing room about personal items that she and John needed.

'Don't you find it humiliating doing this kind of work for us after all the creative things you've done?' she asked. 'You were a movie star.'

'I don't work for you, Yoko, you don't pay me. I do it because I want to. Tittenhurst has been a refuge for us, I've actually been able to stop using heroin. I couldn't have done it without help from you and John.'

'Yes, but you answer the telephone and bring us the mail. Sometimes you talk with Val about how we want our food,' she continued.

'I'm doing a lot of creative work – the record covers, the films, supervising the building of all the creative facilities here.' Her comment hurt and I resented the way she could put you down by putting you on the defensive.

'Sure, but it was all for our projects, never yours.' I was pissed.

John was recording his single *Power to the People*. The Ascot studio was not ready to record in, so we were working at Abbey Road, with Phil Spector producing. Phil was considered a rock and roll genius and John was excited about working with him. Phil had been over in England for a while and had worked with the Beatles on *Let It Be*, and with John and Yoko on the *Plastic Ono Band* albums. John and he had become close and John trusted him creatively. Both John and Phil were both incredibly successful Rock and Roll artists who were evolving away from the styles that had given them their popular successes. Phil's classic *River Deep Mountain High* was not a commercial success in the States, and he had retired only coming back into the studio when the Beatles asked him to produce *Let it Be*. He was a small, frenetic man, and was totally unpredictable. He looked like a dapper nervous pixie in sun glasses. He had a reputation for a need to control that led to stories of brandishing guns and of locking in his wives, girl groups, and children at night. He travelled with a body guard named George Brand who was a retired sheriff's deputy. George was a stocky man with dark hair who wore a black suit and tie. He was both taciturn and friendly, but one sensed a tinge of menace. He was always silently present, keeping Phil both safe and out of trouble.

Yoko did the B-side of the record with her song *Open Your Box*, which naturally drove the 'powers that be' into a frenzy because of its suggestive title. The record was conceived as a two-sided offering rather than the standard A and B side record. I used a Polaroid to take pictures of them both for the covers while we were at Abbey Road. I shot John wearing a fatigue jacket and a construction helmet, like the demonstrators in Japan. His hand was raised in a fist. I shot Yoko attired the same way for her cover with her hand raised in the peace sign. I had now taken the cover photos for three of their albums.

The recording of the chorus was done in the largest Abbey Road studio. Phil brought in Rosetta Hightower and a full gospel chorus to give the record a great sound. As we sat in the control room, John told me a funny story about a time when the Beatles were recording there. They were adding echo to one of their tracks and they keep hearing footsteps on the playback. In turned out, there was a technician doing something inside the echo chamber and it was his footsteps that they were inadvertently recording.

The studio at Ascot was ready enough for us to do the remix, so John and Phil took the master tape back to Tittenhurst and we spent a long night mixing. Everybody was pretty wrecked and at one point Phil really wanted the track, with the chorus singing 'Power to the people,' to pop at the opening. He couldn't get it right, so in desperation, he decided to trim the multi-track master tape. He trimmed more and more off till he and John decided that they had cut too much. They needed to splice back on the last tiny bit of tape they had cut off, but they couldn't find it. The soles of everybody's boots and shoes were examined. The bit of the master tape was actually stuck to one of them, and Phil had it spliced back on to the master. It worked.

The Tittenhurst office was very busy all the time now. We were constantly fielding calls and letters. There were endless requests for interviews, money, support of someone's project, or just an autograph. We were working on films, recordings, interviews, and all kinds of events. On top of this there was John, who was the biggest job we all had. The life of a major rock and roll star was somewhat like that of an Eastern potentate. There was a retinue of retainers who handled affairs down to the tiniest detail. John fell into a very special and rarified niche. No one before the Beatles had sold so many records. Reaching across every demographic, the Beatles touched corners of the world where Western rock and roll had never gone before. The money in music lies in the publishing rights, and since John and Paul had written almost all their songs,

they had amassed staggering fortunes that placed them among the very rich. The fame of the Beatles went far beyond rock and roll. The whole world seemed to want to know what they wore, who they slept with, and their opinion on matters that had absolutely nothing to do with rock. Of all the Beatles, John, from the very start of their career, stood out from the rest. He had an intelligent humour and radical opinions. He had gone to art school, drew pictures, and wrote books.

Sitting cross-legged on his circular bed in Ascot, strumming on his guitar, watching TV, and smoking a joint, John was at the center of an energy vortex that radiated outward from him to the world. Beside him was Yoko, his mentor and consort, on the phone providing spin, damage control, pitching the latest project, conducting the business of John and Yoko.

'John wants . . . John thinks . . . John was very upset with what you wrote . . . '

The next layer was the personal staff and confidents. This was made up of all of us at Tittenhurst: Val; Diana; Stephen; me, the current chamberlain; and Les. We had direct access to John and Yoko, and they for the most part dealt with us directly. If John wanted a couple of crates of Dr Pepper or Yoko needed a box of asparagus over-nighted from Israel, they would ask the inner staff directly. The outer circle at Ascot included Frank and Andy out in the garden and various outside contractors, like Eddie Veale working on the studio and the builders doing the renovations.

Filling John and Yoko's quirky requests led to all kinds of comic events and mutterings but the staff was small, reasonably manageable, and almost like a family.

Then there was a layer made up of the people at and around the Apple office and third-party professionals who serviced the businesses that were the Beatles brand. My favourite of the Apple crowd was the urbane and smart Derek Taylor who was the press officer at Apple when it was still at 3 Savile Row. It was always a pleasure to stop by Derek's office and chat whenever Jill and I were in London. He was an island of sanity and dry humour in the flux and chaos of Apple when it was at Savile Row. Derek had left after Allen Klein became the Beatles' manager and moved the Apple offices to 54 St James Street.

There were the trusted few who were there from the old days, like Neil Aspinall. Neil was a very nice guy who came out of Liverpool with the band in the early days. Describing Neil, John said to me, 'He drove the van.'[6] Then there was Mal. He was the Beatles road manager, the 'King of the Roadies.' Mal shepherded the Beatles through their years of touring.[7] Two other confidants were Tony Bramwell and Terry Doran. Tony had worked on graphics and media since the beginning, and Terry was a good friend of George's.

There were many others, like Tony King who did the A&R. Tony was tall, young, and definitely rock-elegant. Today Tony organises tours for the Rolling Stones. He is a great guy.

Hillary Girard handled Ringo's financial affairs and was a good buddy. He was partial to formal shirts open to the waist with silver chains round his neck dangling sharks' teeth and carnivore claws.

Peter Howard was Allen Klein's ABKO representative. Peter always wore a suit and seemed a bit like a slightly confused visitor

6 After Allen Klein and his ABKO contingent left, Neil ran Apple until his death in 2008.
7 Mal was the Beatles' road manager from the beginning in the summer of 1963. He was twenty-six and working for the Post Office when he discovered the Beatles playing at the Cavern in Liverpool. Mal started hanging out at the Cavern and became friends with George who recommended him as bouncer at the Club. He was there for a short time when Neil Aspinall and the Beatles decided to hire some people to help them out. Mal took over driving the van from Neil and became the Beatles' head roadie. Mal died in a tragic misunderstanding with the police in Los Angeles in 1976.

who was trying to figure out just what these strange people were doing. Les Perrin was the Beatles publicist. There were many others who filled the numerous functions required to keep Apple churning along.

When John needed to move, special problems arose. Speed and secrecy were the best ways to move smoothly. If anyone knew where John would be, the world would know soon after.

Aside from the massive insanity of moving a Beatle through airports and into hotels, there were always the problems presented by dope. In spite of all this, it was always great fun to be with John on an aeroplane. Years of touring had honed his in-flight skills. The one I was most impressed by was how to smoke a joint in the toilet.

'You've got to push down on the lever that opens the drain in the sink so that it sucks the air down. Then, keeping it open, you put your head down in the sink and light the joint, which you've got to keep down right over the drain hole thingy,' he explained. With modern smoke detectors you probably couldn't do it any more, but back then it worked a treat

On flights we took turns to visit the head. There was a lot of giggling and laughing as one of us came back to the seats afterwards. Yoko would give us that 'you're both just being children' look and didn't join in.

Don't Worry, Kyoko

'That's why they are called March hares,' said John as we watched hares leaping high in the air and cavorting in a field next to the small airport on the Isle of Jersey. The hares looked so un-rabbit-like.

'Probably males fighting over the women.' Yoko had a way of seeing the political aspect of things. It was the middle of April 1971. Out on the tarmac our plane was refuelling for the flight to Palma in Majorca. It was a tiny Britten Norman Islander. Our pilot had assured us that we were perfectly safe in the tiny plane, but I didn't like the way it had rocked in the wind as we landed.

Yoko was very distraught; we were travelling to Majorca where she hoped to be able to track down Tony Cox and maybe see Kyoko. The custody battle for Kyoko had dominated the winter and spring. Tony had disappeared with her and Yoko was desperate to find her daughter. John, Yoko, and I had flown down to the south of France to talk with a friend who had been with Tony and Kyoko in a commune in Scandinavia. He told us that Tony had gone to Majorca and he and Kyoko were staying with the Maharishi's people in some unfinished hotels in Manacor on the east side of the island. Yoko was determined to find them.

In Palma, we checked into a wedding cake hotel, a great baroque edifice with a semi-circular drive leading to the front entrance. Once we were settled in, John and Yoko met with a local attorney named Victor Lozano and a young British consular official. Both of them assured Yoko there was nothing to worry about since she had legal custody of Kyoko.

We made two trips across the island to reach Manacor. I rented a car so we could drive without attracting too much attention. On the first trip, Yoko was supposed to wait for someone to escort her to where Kyoko and Tony were. We were left in a room in the unfinished hotel. The building was cheap and tacky, the room sparse with hardly any furniture and light flowing in through the bare windows. Tony had wanted Yoko to come alone, but John wouldn't allow it. He and I decided to hide in the closet so no one would know she was not alone. There was a knock on the door and John and I slipped into the bare closet before Yoko opened the door. We were wedged into this tiny space together listening to the muffled sounds of Yoko talking to whoever was picking her up. We didn't know whether to laugh or be scared. When we heard the door close, we peeked out from the closet. The room was empty.

John and I spent most of the day in the room, talking in whispers so no one passing by would hear us. It was different without Yoko around to drive the conversation. John was relaxed and we talked about our pasts. He asked me about working with Stanley Kubrick and my mime background and what it was like to perform without words. He told me about the craziness of being a touring Beatle with groupies hiding in wait everywhere and the constant offer of sex. In the hotel suites after the concerts, Mal and the other guys travelling with them would act like traffic cops moving the girls in and out of their rooms.

'We became disillusioned with the Maharishi on that trip we all took to stay with "His Holiness" in Rishikesh. We were staying at his ashram where no one was supposed to eat eggs, but when "His Holiness" heard that Ringo wanted eggs for breakfast, he had some flown in by helicopter. What really made me realise that he wasn't as holy as he let on was when he hit on Mia Farrow who was up there with us.'

We both laughed.

'While we were in India, Yoko was writing to me everyday.

What she wrote was more interesting than the stuff the Maharishi was saying. I just wanted to get back to London to see her and talk to her.'

We talked all day; the secrecy of our mission brought us closer together. Up until this time I was Yoko's bohemian friend, hip to the art world, creative, and a dope buddy. John and I had never had the opportunity to relate to each other one on one. That afternoon in Manacor, in that empty room, whispering as the light from the stark windows slowly moved across the floor, our relationship was changing and something more than a sense of fun and humour was born between us. Without the filter of Yoko's presence, barriers had fallen and a seriousness was brought to our friendship. We became friends.

We heard Yoko at the door and she slipped in alone. She had seen Kyoko and had eaten with her in a cafeteria. She had also learned that Kyoko was at a day care centre each morning; she knew the location and when the kids would be outside playing. She had decided she wanted to return the following day and pick up Kyoko from outside the centre.

We had dinner with Victor Lozano in a local restaurant. The walls were panelled with dark wood and the tables covered in rich linen tablecloths. He quietly assured Yoko she had every right to pick up Kyoko since she had legal custody of her.

The next morning, April 24th, I drove the car back to Manacor and pulled up in front of the day care building. I was scared shitless. Yoko, seeing Kyoko playing with the other children, got out of the car, walked purposely over to her and took her hand. As she tried to lead her toward the car, Kyoko became confused and scared and began to cry. Yoko picked her up, jumped into the back seat beside John and we drove away. Things hadn't gone as smoothly as Yoko thought they would and Kyoko was screaming. Yoko and John were trying to calm her. I turned to her and promised everything would be all right and not to be afraid.

On the way back, we approached a spot in the road where some of the Guardia Civil were stopping cars and looking at the occupants. At this point, Kyoko had calmed down, and she, Yoko, and John hunkered down in the back seat and pulled a blanket over themselves. I was scared to death as we pulled up to the roadblock. I put a big smile on my face and we rolled through without being asked to stop. A young Guardia Civil officer wearing one of those funny hats with the brim turned up on one side and a gun slung over his shoulder gave me a suspicious look as I drove past. I wondered if Tony had created some fantastic and grisly story about a violent 'kidnapping.' On the outskirts of Palma, we stopped and called the British consular official and Lozano. They agreed to meet us at the hotel.

When we pulled up in front of the ornate entrance to our hotel, doormen scurried over to hold the car doors and we all got out. There were no police around, so John, Yoko, and Kyoko hurried up to the suite. I went to buy some shoes for Kyoko who was barefoot when Yoko picked her up. When I came back into the lobby with the shoes, there were police, both Guardia Civil and local officers, standing in uniformed groups all around. I went right to a house phone and called up to John and Yoko's suite. John answered the phone.

'The hotel is crawling with fuzz. Don't open the door,' I said.

'Too late, they're already in here,' John said calmly.

The police took John, Yoko, and Kyoko to the main Palma police station. I was afraid that I would be arrested, but I couldn't leave them alone so I went down to the station. I waited an interminable length of time in a large dark anteroom that smelled of dust and tobacco smoke. A bored, middle-aged sergeant sat at an old wood desk behind a long chest-high wooden barrier. He didn't understand any English and my Spanish was terrible. I wanted to get in to make sure John and Yoko were OK. I called Allen Klein in New York, and he said he would send down Peter

Howard from the London office. Peter wouldn't arrive until the morning. The police wouldn't let me in to see John and Yoko, so I had to wait while they were questioned and then taken in front of a judge.

Late at night, they were finally released. I went to them as they came out of the police station. Yoko was devastated and John was trying to soothe her. On the way back to the hotel, John told me that the judge had asked Kyoko whether she wanted to stay with Yoko or go back to Tony. Kyoko said she wanted to be with Tony so the judge let him take her back to Manacor pending a formal hearing.

We knew that as soon as he could, Tony would leave Spain and disappear again with Kyoko. He wouldn't be there for the hearing.

Back at the hotel, we all got some sleep. The next morning was absolute chaos. The story had hit the wires and the hotel was crawling with press and paparazzi. 'What the hell have I gotten myself into?' I asked myself. I was still expecting to be arrested and I knew that John and Yoko, while free, were in real jeopardy of going to jail. We had to leave as soon as possible.

Peter Howard arrived from London and we had a meeting with the lawyers and the British Consular official in John and Yoko's suite. There were all kinds of rumours and stories swirling around. Tony had told the police that John and Yoko had hired Mafia accomplices to do the 'kidnapping.' He was making sure that things looked as bad as he could. I knew Tony, and I knew he would tell the story in such a way as to get enough cover to get out of Spain. Something had to be said to the press so Peter and I went down and held an impromptu press conference. We sat at a table in the front of a ballroom full of shouting press. They asked me about the incident and I make a banal remark about it all being 'a tempest in a teapot.' I felt I was being catapulted into a role that was more than a friend who had just come along for the ride.

Back in the suite with John and Yoko, the attorneys, using arcane

Mediterranean logic, decided there was a window of opportunity while the papers of the case were between Palma and Manacor. They reasoned that, since the incident took place in Manacor, the papers would be on route to a judge there. The case would not come under the jurisdiction of the judge in Palma and would not yet be in the hands of the new judge in Manacor. It sounded pretty sketchy, but we were going to do whatever we could to get John and Yoko out of Spain.

I immediately got on the phone to as many airlines as I could and reserved three seats on every flight out of Palma that day for Mr and Mrs Smith and friend. There was an Air France flight leaving around midday for Paris and we decided to go for it.

It didn't take us very long to pack and soon we were in a gilded birdcage elevator descending to the lobby and possible freedom.

John looked at me and said, 'You have to be on the payroll, Dan. You can't go on not working for us with everything that's happening.'

It didn't seem to be a good time to argue and I thought, 'What the hell; I certainly could use the money.' So I said 'OK' as we stepped out into the ornate lobby.

Somehow we got through the lobby unnoticed and into a car and we were on our way to the little Palma airport without anyone stopping or following us. We were very tense, expecting at any moment to be found out.

The airport was airy and modern and we were able to walk right up to the Air France desk where we picked up three first-class tickets to Paris. Walking to the waiting area, we were trying to look as unobtrusive as possible when suddenly a skinny young man in a tight suit accompanied by two uniformed policemen with rifles walked right up in front of us and looked at John.

'*Signor* Lennon?' he questioned.

I stepped between him and John. John put his arm around Yoko. We were sure we were about to be arrested. 'No, it's Smith,' I said.

'Please come with me,' he said.

Standing there with the sunlight streaming through big windows in the center of the concourse it seemed we were going to be busted.

They led us through a door into a small room.

'You will be more comfortable here, *Signor* Lennon. No one will bother you. I will have someone take you out to your plane as soon as it is ready. In that way you and *Signora* Lennon and your friend can be aboard before the other passengers.'

'Far out,' I thought, 'he is just giving John the VIP treatment.'

We were relieved, but we were still on the ground. A few minutes later, we were escorted out onto the tarmac and up into the aeroplane. An attractive French stewardess sat us up in the front of first class and asked us if we needed anything. We ordered a bottle of champagne but decided not to open it until we were actually in the air. Soon the other passengers boarded the plane, and before long we were taxiing down the runway. John smiled and Yoko visibly began to relax. As the wheels left the ground, we gave a little cheer and opened the champagne. Sipping it, we discussed where we would stay in Paris.

'How about the Georges Cinq?' I said.

Back to Work at Ascot

After a day relaxing in Paris we returned to Ascot. My relationship with John and Yoko had changed. For one thing I was now officially working for them and getting a pay packet. The day I spent with John in that hotel room in Manacor and the events that followed brought us closer together and John had completely accepted me. I had changed from Yoko's helpful friend to John and Yoko's guy. I began to feel the change right away.

'If you're gonna work for us you've got to learn something about rock and roll,' John said to me as he descended the spiral staircase into the sprawling newly finished kitchen.

'Well, John, I know Little Richard, Jerry Lee Lewis, Martha and the Vandelas . . . '

'How about Rosie and the Originals?' He was looking in the big stainless steel fridge for some ice cream.

'Rock and roll is not the most important thing in the world,' mused Yoko, as she settled at the big table to read a letter.

'We've got to fill up the juke box with classics,' he went on as he walked over to the table and sat down beside Yoko. He had brought a gorgeous old Wurlitzer jukebox back from the States. It sat like a multicoloured pop god in the corner of the kitchen, glowing with pastel lights and bubbles rising up through glass tubes along its sides. It was starting to fill with 45s that traced the restless souls of fifties and sixties youth.

As they sat together, they reminded me of mythological archetypes. I was trying to complete the metaphor, Orpheus and Eurydice? That didn't seem to work because Yoko was so strong and I felt at that time they would always be together.

'Don't forget to put some of Phil's songs on the Wurlitzer,' he

146

said as he looked up from the table. John had a great deal of respect for Phil Spector. He used to say that Phil was the greatest of the classic rock and roll producers.

'I've ordered *Da Doo Ron Ron* and all the Crystals[8] and the Ronettes songs I could find,' I replied.

'The rhythm guitar is the heart of rock and roll,' John went on as he dug his spoon into the ice cream. 'It plays in the mid range and establishes the sound, tempo, and rhythm of the song. Rock and roll is mainly heard through a little car speaker in mono. All the highs and lows you hear in the studio are mostly lost when the music comes through that little speaker. That's the way kids are listening to it. That's why the rhythm guitar is so important, and that's what's so cool about Phil. He fills that middle with his "Wall of Sound".'

I watched him sitting there, with Val serving food, Diana bringing papers for him to review, and Stephen with messages from the office. I thought 'he leaves a wake as he travels through the world. As people come closer to him they change like I'm changing. He has an overwhelming effect on everyone around him. They transform just like time and space warps as they come closer to a black hole.' I tried to imagine what it must be like to live inside his head. To look at people and know they couldn't say 'no' to you. To be always beautiful, right and above all, superior.

John had spent most of his life living in a distorted reality. His

8   When Phil Spector discovered the Crystals in 1961, they were fifteen and still in high school in Brooklyn. Lead singer Barbara Alston, Dee Dee Kennibrew, Patsy Wright, Mary Thomas, and Myrna Giraud made their first recording, 'There's No Other (Like My Baby),' with Phil. It is also their first hit, catapulting them straight to the Apollo Theater in Harlem, and the creation of Phil's Philles label. They continued their successful recordings with five more Top Ten records, 'Uptown,' 'He's A Rebel,' 'He's Sure The Boy I Love,' 'Da Doo Ron Ron,' and 'And Then He Kissed Me'. The last two are listed in the Top 50 most popular records in the Rock 'n Roll Hall of Fame.

development and maturity had frozen somewhere back in time as John Lennon the famous Beatle emerged. The little boy abandoned by an indifferent father and unable to live with his mother was left like a butterfly impaled on a pin. To be so loved, adored, worshipped and gifted yet to carry such anger, sense of loss, and feelings of abandonment was somehow more cruel than ironic. I saw this first-hand when he came back from LA after the cathartic work with Art Janov. During the recordings of *The Plastic Ono Band* album he poured out all the feelings the treatment had brought to the surface. Not only did he put these feelings into the album, he often discussed them.

It occurred to me that I had better watch out now I was working for them. I worried that I would find myself falling into the groupie trap. I didn't want to lose the home, the life, the perks, and being part of the life of such a great star. My friend Alex Trocchi had already begun to introduce me as 'Dan Reekter, John Lennon's "yes man".'

I was determined not to flatter. I would try to tell John only the truth.

'Now that you're working for us, we'll have to get you some new clothes,' he said, breaking my reverie.

'What's wrong with the ones I have?'

'Nothing, they look great, you always look cool. Maybe some new stuff would be nice.' He paused, 'I have a couple of things upstairs I could give you. All that stuff from the Apple boutique.'

John always had an eye for clothes. He had a feminine side that cared about clothing and hair, it sort of went with his physical awkwardness. Besides frequently playing with his own hair, he often worked on Yoko's. Once he joked, 'If I hadn't become a rock and roll star, I would have liked to be a hairdresser.'

Later that day, he showed me a floor-length mock-fur coat with a great collar that was definitely dramatic.

'I guess I could wear that,' I said.

'It'll be great on you, you'll see.'

He also brought out some really flamboyant shirts. I liked one that had gigantic blue and yellow flowers on it.

A couple days later, he showed me a jacket he found that was made especially for him by The Fool, the group of artists who had done most of the clothes for the Apple Boutique.

'It's full of pockets,' he said. 'I was always losing things and having other things that I wanted to hide, so I asked them to make me a jacket with lots of pockets.'

It was stunning. Like the fur coat, it also had a big collar. It was made of different coloured velvets and silks. There were pockets all over it. There were pockets on top of pockets and pockets inside of pockets. Some of the pockets were obviously pockets, others were hidden in seams.

'Try it on, it'll look great on you,' John said.

'I can't, John, it was made specially for you.'

'Go ahead, man, I never wear it.'

It was so like John that I felt weird putting it on. As I slipped it over my shoulders, I realised that it fitted perfectly and that I loved it. The jacket was so flamboyant and special that I only wore it occasionally. As time passed and the sixties' styles faded it ended up in a garment bag in the back of my closet. Almost twenty years later, I sold it at Sotheby's to pay for some of Sacha's education.

Politics, Oz, Warhol, and Dylan

I've always been politically minded, you know, and against the status quo. It was pretty basic when you're brought up, like I was, to hate and fear the police as a natural enemy and to despise the army as something that takes everybody away and leaves them dead somewhere.

John Lennon,
from the 1971 *Red Mole* interview with Tariq Ali

Back in 1969, the dreams began to change. The drumbeats of the Manson murders and the murder at the Stones concert at Altamont were the precursors of the end of that shining time when we really believed in our hearts that the world was changing for the better. Freedom turned out not to be the universal panacea we had hoped it would be. Some of us who had turned on, tuned in, and dropped out had become saints while others became monsters and mass murderers. The Hell's Angels were enlisted to provide security at the Stones concert in Altamont. Frenzied with speed and booze, they viciously beat and stabbed a young black man to death. Freedom not only brought out the best in people but the worst. Peace, love, and understanding were coupled with fear, hate, murder, and racism. When Thomas de Quincy, who wrote The *Confessions of an English Opium-Eater,* was asked what it was like to take opium, he suggested that if a man 'whose talk is of oxen' should become an opium-eater, the probability is that he will dream about oxen. And so it was with us. The drugs had made each of us more of who we were already. So by 1969 we found ourselves ranging from saints and visionaries to mass murderers. During the following years many hippies and beatniks tried to deal with this in many ways, from abandoning the cities for communes and religious communities to political activism.

Rock'n roll stars are constantly in the spotlight, receiving bushels of mail, endless phone calls, and giving endless interviews to facile, trend-following reporters. They become acutely aware of the *zeitgeist* and every nuance and fluctuation of trends. A strange symbiosis seems to take place where what they say and do is either creating or following a trend. John and Yoko were like litmus paper reflecting the changes as they happened. From two hippie saints dressed in white with garlands of flowers singing 'Give Peace a Chance' in their wedding beds, they had morphed into political activists dressed in fatigues jackets with construction helmets and raised fists. *Give Peace a Chance* had become *Power to the People.* So as the times changed John and Yoko changed. I felt a strange disconnect watching them. I have always gone my own way, often to my detriment. Perhaps it came from growing up in a family with strong commitments to their own values separate from the current trends. It also occurred to me that while we were now friends and I was in their favour, the day might come when they would tire of me and I would be left behind as they moved on to the next and the next.

During the spring of 1971 life at Ascot was becoming very political. The peace period had changed into a more radical phase with John and Yoko dressed in black leather and army surplus. For interviews they wore construction helmets like the young Japanese anti-war demonstrators. They were making stronger pronouncements against the war in Vietnam and the troubles in Northern Ireland. Tariq Ali, the young intellectual and radical socialist, and his partner Robin Blackburn came to Ascot to do an interview with Yoko and John for Tariq's revolutionary magazine, *Red Mole.*

Richard Neville, Jim Anderson, and Felix Dennis, published a psychedelic counter-culture magazine named *Oz.* It was a satirical, colourful and irreverent vehicle for the hip scene with regular contributors like the American cartoonist R. Crumb. They put out a 'School Kids' issue' with kids between the ages of fourteen and eighteen and a great deal of space was devoted to their writings about pop music, sexual freedom, hypocrisy, drug use, corporal punishment and exams. The publishers were prosecuted and convicted on obscenity charges.

John and Yoko invited down a colourful crowd of volunteers who were mounting a campaign to help appeal the convictions. We fixed up the Tudor Lodge, down at the bottom of the garden to house them all. A Gestetner copying machine was installed to help them generate publicity.

They were a flamboyant bunch, including Felix Dennis and a group of Australians from a commune. One fellow wore a T-shirt showing an erect penis with butterfly wings.

John wrote the songs *God Save Us* and *Do the Oz* to raise money for them. He recorded the songs at Ascot in the unfinished studio with the help of Ringo, Phil Spector, Klaus Voorman and Mal Evans. Stephen Brendell played congas and I manned the board in the recording studio with Yoko advising. To get around contractual complications, John decided to overdub his voice on the A-side of 'Do the Oz' with that of Bill Eliot from a band called Half breed that Mal knew. I took the photo of Bill Eliot for my fourth record cover.

Even though the politics of the time were dreadfully serious, a party atmosphere seemed to pervade everything we did. The heady sense of change and freedom that filled the air exhilarated us all.

Peter Bendrey returned once again from India. He found my telephone number and address through Alex Trocchi.

'Hey man, it's so good to hear your voice,' I said to Peter as we talked on the phone. 'What you gonna do?'

'I don't know, man. I need to find a job,' he said.

'Let's get you a job out here,' I said. 'John and Yoko would love to see you.'

'That would be great, man. I can make tea and see to their whims. As I told them before I left for India, I am the perfect body servant.' We both laughed.

Peter arrived the next day in sandals and with his hair still in a ponytail. He was carrying a large sitar, an Indian stringed instrument. John and Yoko were very happy to see him and he fitted right into our life at Tittenhurst.

Desirée, the wife of Michael X, had also come to stay at Ascot. Desirée was a small, soft-spoken and dignified lady. Michael had recently been released from jail and left England for what he hoped would be the safety of Trinidad. He had many enemies, many of them in high places and was concerned for Desirée's safety. John and Yoko offered to let Desirée stay at Ascot until he was settled in Trinidad.

Things were heating up.

Back in New York, John's naivety continued to surprise me. When we visited Yoko's artist friends, he was almost sheepish. This guy, who was one of the most successful musical artists ever, wanted to be accepted as something more than a rock star. He was constantly trying to become more sophisticated. He never forgot that he came from a working-class home in provincial Liverpool. Being around him all the time, I never saw any lack in him. He had a worldliness gained from living through the Beatle experience. He was keenly intelligent and humorous, and above all, unique. Every now and then, you meet someone like that, someone completely himself, not like anyone else at all. Sure, he didn't know much about a bunch of fringe avant-garde artists and he only had a spotty high school education, but so what? Sometimes I felt that Yoko was using his innate insecurities to gain a kind of power over him. I think he wanted her to do that, too. He had a passive side that she brought out. He wanted to be told that he didn't know things and that he should do this or that. I had the feeling it went back to being unable to live with his mother. He said he never had a chance to mature like the rest of us because he was swept up into being a Beatle and touring while still a teenager.

New York was Yoko's territory and she was John's Virgil, leading him through the world of the underground and avant-garde arts. A typical visit had the three of us in the limo driving down to Soho and beyond to meet someone in a bare loft who had worked with or known Yoko years before.

Yoko was always explaining to John the nuances of conceptual art and where each artist we visited fit into it all. One thing everyone had in common was that they were poor. Most conceptual artists live off grants or patrons, so you can imagine what it was like making tea in your barren loft for multimillionaires when one was the most famous rock star in the world and the other was an old friend.

We would leave the opulence of the Plaza and midtown and weave down the west side, past darkened docks.

'So, this is where guys fuck each other in the ass in the back of trucks,' John observed as we passed below Chelsea.

George Macunias was one of the founders of Fluxus that we visited a couple of times. He was skinny, intelligent and spoke rapidly with an Eastern European accent. George made pancakes on a single burner hot plate for us.

It seemed as though John was intrigued by meeting artists who were totally devoted to what they were doing even though they were on the outer fringe of the art world and grindingly poor. This was more real to him than the world of money, adulation, and fame that he was used to.[9]

One day we were supposed to meet Bob Dylan at the Plaza. As we approached the hotel, I asked the driver to stop at the door on the park side where Trader Vic's restaurant used to be. I got out

---

9 Some of the visits produced recordings like the one John and Yoko produced of the music of conceptualist Henry Flynt.

first and looked around. The coast seemed clear, no fans and no suspicious people. I told John and Yoko it was OK to get out, and we entered the lobby and walked toward the elevator. Suddenly, a large man moved purposely toward us and looked like he was reaching inside his jacket. As he approached us, he said, 'Mr Lennon?'

I stepped between John and the large man, putting my hands up, saying, 'Talk to me.' I was scared shitless. The guy looked like Jack Ruby and I was sure something really bad was about to happen. Stopping in front of me, he said, 'Hotel security. Is this Mr Lennon?' The idiot wanted to help. Half the time, guys like him ended up asking John for autographs for their kids.

I wanted to kill him. I mumbled something like, 'Thanks, we're fine,' as we stepped into an open elevator.

A nondescript, slight man in an old army jacket, floppy hat pulled down over his eyes and a big smile on his face slipped into the elevator beside us and said 'Hi.' Bob Dylan had been watching it all as he waited anonymously for Yoko and John in the lobby.

We all went up to one of the rooms and, sitting on two of the beds, we smoked a really fat joint I rolled with hash sprinkled over grass. I don't remember a word we said.

One day John and Yoko arranged a meeting with Andy Warhol. They were determined to be treated as serious artists and were looking forward to meeting him. Andy floated into their suite wearing blue jeans and a blazer. With wimpy insouciance and a half smile, he said 'Hello' and we sat around for a bit discussing John and Yoko's projects. Andy had an easy way of drawing people out. Soon we all went over to the Pierre for lunch. Sitting in a banquette, Andy asked John and Yoko question after question and responded with phrases like, 'Oh really? What was that like?'

About halfway through lunch, Andy said, 'I'd love to interview you for my magazine *Interview*. Do I have permission to record you?'

John and Yoko looked at each other and John said, 'Sure.'

'Oh, that's good because I already have. 'He reached down on the seat beside him and picked up a little Sony cassette recorder. He put it up on the table and muttered something like, 'This will be great in *Interview*.'

Andy had a Polaroid camera with a long nose that was made for portraits. He showed John and Yoko how he could take a picture and then, instead of pulling the Polaroid out, take another picture. When he pulled it out, he had a double exposure. This was the technique Yoko would use to take a double exposure of John's head with clouds that we ended up using for the cover of Imagine.

Andy said he wanted to do a portrait of John and Yoko. Yoko suggested that they do a portrait of him. Andy thought that would be great.

'Call Fred – he works out all the details for me on things like that,' he said.

The next day, I called Fred who told me that John and Yoko would have to pay Andy about $40,000 for the portrait. When I told Fred they had expected to exchange portraits, Fred said, 'Oh no, Andy's work is worth so much more than John and Yoko's.'

Mr Buckley, I Presume?

It was getting harder and harder for John to get into the States. He and Yoko were lobbying many people they thought could help them. John really wanted to be able to live there without a constant hassle. One of the strangest trips I ever made for them had to do with lobbying. I flew to Switzerland to see, of all people, William F. Buckley.

The drug bust at George's London flat at 34 Montague Square on October 18, 1968, now standing in the way of John obtaining a US visa, was a plant. Jimi Hendrix had been staying there before he and Yoko rented it from George, and John, having been tipped off that Piltcher was after him, had the flat meticulously cleaned. When he opened the door to the police he knew there was nothing there. Sergeant Pilcher was prepared – he had brought some hashish in a matchbox that he conveniently 'found' in a binocular case on the mantelpiece. He then proceeded to arrest John and Yoko. Yoko was pregnant so John decided to plead guilty to avoid putting her through the stress of a trial. He told me that he was so worried that she might miscarry that he got the whole thing over as quickly as possible. Sadly, Yoko eventually did miscarry. That guilty plea now had severe ramifications. The US government, and particularly the Nixon administration, was using it to justify denying him even a visitors visa.

Ironically, on November 8, 1973, Sergeant Norman Pilcher was found guilty of conspiracy to pervert the course of justice for planting the drugs. He was sentenced to four years in prison.

On one of our trips to New York, John and Yoko had several meetings with people who might be able to influence the government. Yoko was on the phone all the time, lobbying whomever would talk to her. We met with a representative of the Kennedy family at the Plaza. It seemed a little incongruous for them to be currying favour with the establishment, but after all, they were very rich as well as very famous.

In Ascot, Yoko asked me to take a letter to William Buckley. She had talked to him on the phone about helping with John's case. I flew from London to Geneva with a letter for Mr Buckley in the pocket of my black velvet jacket.

The more John was harassed about being able to visit or live in the States, the more he wanted to do it. New York was perfect for him. He was a rock and roll musician and America was the home of rock and roll.

'It's open 24 hours,' he said. Musicians live at different hours from other people, working long into the night when the rest of us are asleep.

Living in the States also appealed to John because he loved to watch TV. It was more than entertainment or a distraction for him. It was information for his insatiable mind. England only had three channels, BBC One, BBC Two, and ITV. It was pretty limited and staid by American standards.

Yoko didn't tell me much about the letter I was carrying to Buckley. I knew he had agreed to help with lobbying the US government to ease up on John. His brother Jim was a US Senator and had close contacts with the Nixon administration. It still seemed a bit strange for a rock and roll radical to be communicating with an arch-conservative like Buckley. Knowing John, I knew he wouldn't stop saying what he believed. The more he and Yoko talked about peace and called for an end to the Vietnam War, the more concerned the Nixon administration became. That was the issue – the drug bust was just an excuse to keep two highly vocal antiwar radicals out of the States.

Yoko explained that her sister Setsko, who lived in Geneva, would meet me at the airport. She had arranged for a car to drive me to Berne. From there a short drive to the little cable car would take me up to the hotel where I was to meet Buckley.

I liked Setsko; she was an intelligent, pleasant, and soft-spoken young lady. She didn't have any of Yoko's radical bohemian qualities. It was as if they had come from different families. She had the manners of the wealthy aristocracy.

Setsko met me at the airport in Geneva as promised. She had hired a chauffeur-driven black Mercedes for me. As I climbed into the back of the car, the chauffeur informed me that he would have to drive very fast in order to catch the last cable car of the day up to the hotel.

'Go for it,' I said, as I thanked Setsko and said goodbye.

We immediately set off at a hair-raising speed along the north shore of Lake Geneva. We were driving to Murren, a little hamlet high in the Bernese Oberland. I dozed fitfully as we sped along.

The driver somehow got me to the cable car in time. I checked the schedule as I jumped on it, and told him to meet me the next day at around noon.

The cable car carried me high above the valley to a idyllic little village which looked like a kitschy Swiss postcard. I must have cut a strange figure as I walked to the hotel, picking my way through the snow in my handmade black leather Russian dancing boots. I crunched and slipped along, pulling the jacket of my black velvet, suit closed over my flimsy silk shirt. With the other hand, I held onto my black Stetson cowboy hat. Through my little wire-framed sunglasses, I could see the prim Swiss locals staring at me.

The hotel was a chalet with overhanging eaves. Smoke rose from its chimney. Inside, I checked into my room and then, making sure the letter was in my pocket, I went down to dinner.

Mr Buckley was sitting with a small group of very conservative-looking older people. I waited for him to get up and go into the hall.

'Mr Buckley?' I asked. I must have appeared a bit strange to him in my sixties hippie garb. He jumped when he saw me but was very friendly once I introduced myself. I told him I would be in the hotel until just before noon the next day if he wanted to send a reply. And with that, we parted.

The next morning was a gorgeous day. I climbed up onto a ridge overlooking the Aletsch glacier and sat looking across at the three great peaks, the Jungfrau, the Eiger, and the Mönch. I had climbed the Mönch a few days before my twelfth birthday. It had been a long journey from those years when I was a kid with a passion to climb mountains. I smoked a joint and pondered the irony of secret communications between leaders of the radical movement and the conservative elite. I guess money is more of a common factor than politics.

Buckley did not have a return message for me, so I caught the cable car down and arrived back in Ascot that night.

He later said that he asked his brother Jim, a US senator at the time, to see if he could persuade the feds to go easy on John. I remember thinking that when John and Yoko retreated into the Dakota and gave up their radical activism, could it have been part of a deal they made in exchange for permission to stay.

Back in Ascot things were moving along in their normal rock and roll rhythm. Everyone was talking about Mick Jagger marrying Bianca Perez Morena de Macias. John and Yoko put together a gift for Mick and Bianca's wedding. One of Yoko's art pieces was a clock with no hands. At Yoko's request, we bought a gold clock from Asprey's in London and had the hands removed. It was sent to Mick and Bianca as a wedding present.

I was so busy that I hardly noticed how well my recovery was going. Work, no heroin, money and time to paint in the evening had me thinking I was ready to get my career back on track as soon as an opportunity presented itself.

Cannes – The Fortnight of the Directors

Louis Malle looked up at Jeanne Moreau and, pointing to me, said, 'Jeanne, this is Dan and he is madly in love with you. You must kiss him.'

I had just told everyone that my favourite French star was Jeanne and that I had fallen completely in love with her when I saw her in *Jules et Jim.*

Jeanne bent over and planted a kiss right on my mouth. Everyone laughed as I turned bright red.

Yoko, John, and I were sitting with Louis and his brother Vincent on the terrace of the Carlton hotel during the Cannes Film Festival. It was the second week in May 1971. We had come to Cannes for screenings of John and Yoko's films at the *Quinzaine des Realisateurs*, the Fortnight of the Directors. The Fortnight had been formed a few years earlier by angry filmmakers such as François Truffaut and Jean-Luc Godard. It was a radical and experimental side-bar to the Festival. The filmmakers were angry because Henri Langlois had been evicted as Director of the Cinémathèque Française in Paris. They decided to form a noncompetitive fortnight, without censorship or diplomatic considerations, to serve as a showcase for all international film industries. It was a perfect venue for John and Yoko's films, as well a major focus of the energy of the art scene.

We were screening John's film *Apotheosis*, an 18-minute camera shot from a balloon rising through the clouds above a snowy countryside, and Yoko's *Fly*. Vincent Malle was a distributor, and we were getting to know him and Louis with the hope that they could help John and Yoko get distribution for their films.

John and Yoko were energised by our experiences in New York creating Up *Your Legs Forever* and *Fly*. They were developing a significant body of work and were encouraged by the reception it was getting. Andy Warhol was getting distribution for his films and the times seem right for John and Yoko to do the same. We had all been scurrying around at Ascot in an attempt to organise their trip to Cannes. We had made contact with Charlie Chaplin's people and they arranged for John and Yoko to have a sumptuous suite of rooms at the Hotel du Cap in Cap d'Antibes close to Cannes. Chaplin had reserved this ornate beauty but would not be using it. I had a shoulder bag stuffed with press materials we had put together, and John, Yoko, and I arrived in Cannes with a shortened version of *Fly* and a print of *Apotheosis*.

Cannes was alive with *avant-garde* energy. Richard Dembo, a young French filmmaker, acted as our publicist and John and Yoko were holding court and meeting all sorts of folks. The screening of *Fly* was a great success and received a standing ovation. It was great meeting so many famous and interesting people. Howard Smith, the *Village Voice* columnist, was there with his film about the evangelist Marjoe Gortner. Also from the *Village Voice* was the zany Jill Johnson, as well as Jim Haynes, who, like Johnny Appleseed, moved from festival to festival with his latest underground magazine, *Suck*. Susan Sontag had a film in the Fortnight and we sat with her discussing what feminism and just about everything else meant. We also made friends with Barbara Loden, wife of Elia Kazan. On a later trip to New York, Barbara let me make a finer cut of *Fly* in the editing room at her and Kazan's brownstone.

Everyone wanted to meet John, and for Yoko, the Fortnight was a perfect venue as she already had a reputation as an *avant-garde* filmmaker. Everywhere we went – restaurants, at the screenings, sitting in cafes – people wanted to talk to them about their films.

The energy was fantastic. John decided that with all the publicity they were generating and the famous people we were meeting, I needed to look smarter. He took me into a local men's store and picked out a flamboyant lavender denim jacket. I called Stephen Brendell, at the Tittenhurst office, and he drove down with some 'War is Over' T-shirts. On the way he was involved in an accident, but still made it in one piece. Diana Robertson flew down and checked into the hotel with us. She helped with all the administrative work that was being generated.

John and I developed a game centred on the stealing of ashtrays. It began quite harmlessly with an ashtray from a restaurant or hotel slipped into a pocket but soon got out of hand. We kept trying to top each other, and soon the game turned into how big an ashtray we could each steal. One afternoon, Al Aronowitz the rock columnist was interviewing John and Yoko in a hotel lobby. I saw a really big glass ashtray on a side table and slipped it under my new lavender coat. Standing so that only John could see me, I caught his eye and slowly opened my coat to reveal the ashtray. Without missing a beat, John excused himself to Al, got up, and disappeared into the men's room. Minutes later, he came back with a gigantic ashtray that he handed to me as he returned to the interview.

'I just talked to Keith on the phone.'

John was referring to Keith Richard. Keith had invited him and Yoko over to a house he was renting on Cap-Ferrat, across the water from Villefranche just down the coast from Cannes.

On a beautiful spring night the three of us climbed into a rented car. I drove along the coast toward Nice with the hope that Keith might have some decent dope. I was still clean of heroin and pretty stable on Methadone, but the addict's denial was starting to show its head and the thought of a one-time treat seemed pretty attractive to me.

As we approached the high walls and iron gates, I could see two guys sitting on chairs with guns on their laps, making sure only friends entered.

Driving up the winding drive, we saw the great house set back on lawns that swept down to the water, across from the lights of Villefranche and the Riviera coast. It was all lit up, with rows of French doors open to the June air. Through the doors, lace curtains floated in the breeze and I thought of *The Great Gatsby*. Instead of the strains of jazz, we hear the pounding beat of Jerry Lee Lewis as we pulled up in front of the main entrance.

Keith and John were happy to see each other and the talk immediately turned to dope. Keith told us that his guy, Spanish Tony, was sick and kicking in a back bedroom so he wouldn't be able to help us. He motioned for me to go into the living room and he and John and Yoko disappeared upstairs to talk.

The main room was filled with all kinds of people partying and listening to Jerry Lee Lewis. A girl who looked like an Afro-English model floated up and handed me a joint. She was gorgeous. She had her hair in pigtails and was wearing what looked like a little girl's pinafore, only very sheer and transparent. She had a gigantic lollypop in her hand. This was going to be fun, I thought.

Just as I was settling in, John and Yoko came down with Keith and said that they had to leave because John wasn't feeling well. As we moved toward the door, John went into the bathroom by the door and vomited. We hurriedly said goodbye to Keith, and Yoko and I got John into the car. I wondered whether the Spanish Tony being sick story was really true; I assumed John and Yoko did get some dope from Keith.

We drove up to St Paul de Vence to eat at the famous country inn, the Colombe d'Or. Driving along the roads in the hills behind Cannes was fantastic. The French countryside was green, lush, and beautifully manicured. St Paul de Vence was up near Grasse, famous for lace making. It was just over a half-hour's drive inland from Cannes. There was a bunch of us in the garden of this wonderful restaurant with its golden light, superb food, fig trees, and paintings. A fabulous private collection of paintings by Picasso, Matisse, and Braque hung on the walls. The artists used to trade their work for a meal or a bed. We sat down to a delightful luncheon.

Afterwards we waited outside in the afternoon sun for the car. In the little square, old men gossiped and played the local bowling game *Petanque* with steel *boules*.

Back in Ascot, the lawyers approached me to go down to Palma to meet with a judge. They said he was prepared to settle and drop the kidnapping case. The lawyers were assuring me that I was in no danger, but I wasn't sure I believed them.

I took Jill and Sacha with me to Palma and we checked into the same hotel where John and Yoko had been arrested. With the help of local attorneys, I cleaned up my image. I got a short haircut and bought a dark blue suit, black shoes, a white shirt, and a tie. Just so I wouldn't feel I had abandoned my hip style, the shirt was *bordado* with white embroidery on the front.

I met the judge in his wood-panelled chambers. He asked me a few perfunctory questions and seemed satisfied with my answers. After the meeting, the attorneys told me that money had changed hands, all arrangements had been made, and the case dropped. Then they told me that the charges against me had also been dropped. I was furious. No one had informed me that I had been charged with anything. I had come back into Spanish jurisdiction without knowing I was in jeopardy and had brought my pregnant wife and my three-year-old son with me.

Pissed off about having been tricked into going to Palma, I decided to take a week off in Marrakech at the La Mamounia Hotel with Jill and Sacha. The La Mamounia was one of three great colonial hotels along with Raffles in Singapore and the Sheppard's Hotel in Cairo. It was a palace of art deco and Moorish design, surrounded by idyllic gardens that were almost three hundred years old. The halls and rooms were covered in Moroccan tile and there were fountains everywhere and doves in the garden. Not wanting to talk to John and Yoko, I called Diana and gave her the telephone number and telex.

'When will you be back?' she asked.

'I don't know,' I replied.

Recording *Imagine*

The John and Yokofication of Tittenhurst was just about complete. We had a little bit of wiring to do in the studio, but the renovation of the main house was really done. It was beautiful and everything was operational; the studio, the editing room, the darkroom. Outside, the grounds were lush with spring colours and the lake was complete. It was a perfect setting for John and Yoko to make John's next album.

On a gorgeous morning in June 1971 I was talking with John and Yoko in their bedroom at Tittenhurst.

'Tell Eddie Veale to have the studio ready tonight. I'll call Mr Harrison and Mr Starkey to tell them that I'm going to record tonight.' John was sitting cross-legged in the middle of the big round bed at Ascot with an acoustic guitar in his lap. Yoko was sorting through the mail I had just brought up.

'Uh . . . the studio is still not completely ready,' I said. My mind was racing to work out how we could finish it in time.

'You can do it,' he said with a smile. 'Oh, and don't forget to call Mal.'

It happened just like that. Eddie Veale, the studio designer, and I worked feverishly to get it ready. During that week, John planned to make his and Yoko's vision of breaking free from the constraints of Apple, the Beatles, and rock and roll stardom become a reality. The album was going to be called *Imagine* and would be completely created at Tittenhurst. It began as an angry response to Paul *McCartney's* album *Ram*. John not only wanted to respond to the songs in which he felt Paul was attacking him, but more than *anything*, he wanted to show the world that he could make a mainstream album on his own that would be a major success.

Since the Beatles began the prolonged process of the break up, all the work he and Yoko created had not sold like the Beatles songs did. The conceptual work, like *Life With the Lions* and Yoko's work, had not sold well at all. I could feel the tension between him and Yoko. Up till then they had done everything together and the style was dominated by Yoko's conceptualism. But what Paul called 'the divorce' had really heated up and John was pissed and wanted to show what he could really do. He had Diana working on a list of the Lennon-McCartney songs, dividing them up into those that were his and those that were Paul's. The fact that, everywhere he went, he heard Paul's *Yesterday* really rankled him. People were saying he couldn't do mainstream music without Paul.

'The Beatles was my band. Paul auditioned for me,' he said. He wanted to make it clear that he chose to work with Yoko on conceptual stuff, but if he wanted to, he could create a successful mainstream album. *Imagine* would be it.

'Dan, hand me that soldering iron.' Eddie Veale was under the big console in the recording studio. We had spent the day twisting and soldering wires, getting everything as ready as we could.

As I handed Eddie the soldering iron, there was a knock on the big front door. I heard Val answer it, followed by the voice of Mal Evans getting louder as he approached the studio.

Getting up, I greeted Mal who was standing in the door. Mal was a gigantic man, an even-tempered, bearded teddy bear.

'I thought this might come in handy.' Mal handed me half a kilo of primo black Afghani hash.

'Excellent,' I said, 'let's test it.'

It was already early evening and soon Klaus Voorman and the other musicians began to arrive. June days are long in England and it was still light. As the light began to fade you could hear the sounds of the instruments tuning up and the studio began to come to life. Hearing the sounds from the studio, John and Yoko came down and as John greeted Klaus and the others I could see that he was very nervous. This was the first time he was going to record an album that was all his work in his own private studio. Ascot was his home and he was in control, but this album was special. It wasn't just Paul and the break-up; it was because John had grown so much as a person and an artist. *Imagine* was written for everyone, for the whole world, and embodied all the ideas and principles that he and Yoko had been expressing as well as the deep feelings that had been uncovered during the Primal Scream therapy. None of us could have known that night that it would be John's masterpiece, but we knew that it was going to be very special.

George Harrison, who was still on good terms with both John and Paul, was going to play lead guitar. He hadn't arrived yet and Phil Spector, who was supposed to be producing, hadn't turned up either. John was hoping that George would arrive soon, but everyone expected Phil to be late. John wasn't going to wait for Phil and, with a young engineer named Eddie Offord at the recording console, he set right to work. We all went into the control room and it was amazing to see how easily John began to work. He just started to make the album track by track. He needed the rhythm tracks first and showed Klaus exactly how he wanted the bass to play. It was coming right from his head, as he had very little written down. He knew how he wanted every part of each song to be. He and Yoko must have worked it all out beforehand. She, for her part, was actively involved helping and advising at every turn. Soon we were laying down tracks on the big brand new Studer 8-track recorder.

A while later, the front door bell rang; I walked through the kitchen into the white section of the mansion to answer the door.

'Hi, Dan, can I come in?' George was standing there holding his guitar in a case.

'Sure, George, come on in.'

'Has he started?' he asked.

'Yeah, he's laying down some rhythm tracks with Klaus.'

'Is there somewhere I can go so I that I can play on my own for a bit?'

I took George into one of the front rooms of the white section and left him to warm up. Back in the studio, John asked me if he had arrived.

'Yeah, he's warming up.'

Over the next week at Ascot, John recorded *Imagine*. He used a number of great musicians, among them Alan White and Jim Gordon on the drums, Nicky Hopkins on the electric piano, and John Barham on the harmonium and vibes. John played the rhythm guitar and he played the big white Steinway on *Imagine*. George played lead guitar. Steven Brendell helped out on the maracas.

It was very illuminating to watch John when he was really in his element. In the conceptual art world, he was still a neophyte, constantly deferring to Yoko, but here he was the consummate professional and in complete control. Yoko was his partner – advising, suggesting, and in every way, his creative equal. John and Yoko's keen intelligence and creativity combined synergistically and the work went quickly and decisively. I never saw John reaching for things; you had the feeling that it was all in his head in great detail. Years of performing, touring, and recording had obviously honed his skills. We were talking one day about how fast he worked and he told me how he and Paul wrote *I Want to Hold Your Hand*. It was in the fall of 1963, and they needed a song to break into the American market. They were sitting side by side at a piano in the basement of Jane Asher's house, and Paul hit an E minor chord and from that he said they wrote the song in about an half an hour.

The real surprise came when it was time for him to record the voice tracks. His singing was so genuine and intense that I was stunned at first. Having taught mime and acting, at the American Academy of Dramatic Arts and the American Mime Theatre, I was very aware of what we call 'acting values'. We spent hours in the classroom trying to get students to use parts of themselves to bring a sense of truth to their work. Most never even got close.

'It's so personal, he's so real,' Peter Bendrey whispered to me. He had just come into the studio with some food for Yoko while John was singing 'Crippled Inside' and had stayed to roll a fat joint and listen. It was a song about Paul.

'Yeah, he's so vulnerable, so real. How the fuck does he do it?'

'Beats me, man. I guess it's because he was a Beatle,' said Peter, passing the joint.

'Yeah, but the other Beatles can't sing like that.'

We were sitting in the studio, after working all night without the man who was supposed to be producing the album with John and Yoko. A limo pulled up in front of the mansion. In the back sat Phil Spector and Dennis Hopper. Phil was shit-faced and Dennis had already passed out. Phil needed help with Dennis who was wet with what we hoped was spilt beer. Mal and some of the guys carried Dennis in and put him on a couch in the back of the studio while Phil set to work.

Phil was diminutive and frenetic. He looked like a skinny elf. He immediately seemed to sober up and set to work as if he had been there all along. Dennis slept soundly on the couch. Over the next week, I saw a lot more of Phil and, as he worked, I began to see why John had so much respect for him. He took complete control which left John free to perform. Phil's bodyguard, a gentleman I only knew as George, sat in an adjacent room wearing a dark suit and tie. George was soft-spoken and quite amiable. He seemed such a contrast to the flamboyant Phil.

Yoko was completely supportive of John and constantly helped with creative and practical suggestions. Yoko had a musical education and was able to write down the musical notation as John recorded it. I wished all those critics who characterised her as an opportunist Japanese actress could have seen her.

The cinematographer Nic Knowland and his crew came in to

film some of the recording. The footage Nic shot during the recording period was the beginning of what John and Yoko planned to make into the film *Imagine*. We started in the studio, shooting the standard close-ups of John singing into the mike.

'I want to play *Imagine* in the big white room,' said John.

It could be great footage. John was referring to the white front room where the big white Steinway piano was the only piece of furniture. The room was painted entirely white, had a white marble fireplace, and some of Yoko's art pieces on white pedestals. The floor was covered by white carpet. John and Yoko decided that John should sit at the piano playing as he sang *Imagine*. They wanted the shot to begin with Yoko, dressed in one of the robes Jill had bought for her, slowly opening the white wooden shutters that covered the big French doors lining the outside wall of the room. As the shot progressed, the room would slowly fill with light and then Yoko would go over to John and end up sitting beside him at the piano. The song was a vision of what the world could be if all the ideas that John and Yoko were talking about became a reality.

In order to get the shot, we had to run wires to the mikes and John's headphones from the studio. He needed his headphones so he could hear the playback of the backing tracks. The wires had to run across the work area, through the kitchen, through the white area, and then on to where John was sitting at the piano. We got lots of cable and were able to get the mikes for John and the piano and his headphones working. The problem was that the piano was just slightly out of tune with the instruments that had already been recorded. For a while, John considered over-dubbing one of the electric pianos in the studio, but it just didn't sound right. With the help of Eddie Veale we solved the problem by subtly adjusting the speed of the one of the tape recorders.

Now that the recording and the final mixes were done, the last problem was the pig. Paul had a picture on his *Ram* album of him holding a ram by the horns. John wanted to be photographed holding a large pig by the ears as a response to Paul. It sounded like an easy enough idea, so we arranged for a local farmer to bring by a very big pig and we had a photographer waiting. We had the pig led to an appropriate spot out on one of the lawns and John came out for the photograph. He took one look at the big, smelly, and uncooperative pig and turned white. He daintily approached the pig that the farmer was holding and gingerly reached out to take a hold of it in a pose to mimic Paul's photo. He got even more nervous as he realised that the farmer would have to let go of the pig in order to get out of the picture. We tried a number of times to get a picture we could use and finally John's anger at Paul overcame his fear of the pig and we got the shot.

Filming *Imagine*

This was a halcyon period at Ascot. John and Yoko's films were being shown all over. John's *Imagine* album was energising both of them. During their trips to New York, they were lionised and recognised as stars in the pantheon of leaders in the peace movement. For a period of almost a month starting during the recording of the album, daily life at Ascot was taken up with the making of their film of *Imagine.* They wanted to augment the studio footage and the scene of John playing the white piano while singing *Imagine* in the white room.

Each day Yoko and John came down from their bedroom dressed as their latest manifestation. Yoko often had extreme décolletage and wore black or white short shorts, which we all found a bit humorous and definitely un-conceptual artist-like. John had a flat-rimmed Spanish black cowboy hat that he often wore. John chewed gum, wore his yellow tinted glasses, and smoked his Gauloises.

For days they were cavorting about dressed like Errol Flynn and Rita Hayworth, while the crew and I shot them in various scenes. I could never figure out why they chose to look that way except that they were having a spoof and having a lot of fun.

They seemed more like kids than rock and roll stars as we worked. They were having fun. It seemed that times like this always energised them. They were indulging their creativity and the out-pouring was just plain fun.

'Just get this part of my face.'

John was sitting in a chair beside the house and was explaining to me how to shoot a close-up of his face. I was taking a portrait of him that we were going to use for the cover of *Imagine.* Yoko was directing everything from behind me and the camera crew was shooting all three of us for the movie. Yoko had conceived of an image for the cover of the album of John's head with clouds in his eyes, so they had asked me to design something.

I took my head shot of John and printed it large and then set to work with an X-Acto knife, cutting out clouds and pasting them over his eyes. I liked the idea, but the clouds always seem too small no matter how I arranged them.

Nick shot us as I was showing John and Yoko some of my results.

I ended up walking through many of the scenes in the film dressed in a long dark-blue Moroccan burnoose of Jill's. In one scene, I was serving them tea on a balcony patio; in another, I was driving them down to John's lake in a big black Austen Princess hearse that they had bought. The symbolism eluded me and they never really explained what they were doing. They made remarks like, 'Wouldn't it be cool to have you wearing the robe and driving us as Errol and Rita down to the lake?'

At one point, they had a very nervous Diana climbing a ladder up to a roof where we had the office. Once on the roof, she arrived at a piece of Yoko's that was a sponge with a dropper. Diana put drops of water on the sponge from the eye-dropper.

In the midst of all this, another drama was beginning to unfold. One day Diana came to me with a telegram we had received that was simply signed 'Claudio,' saying that John was sending messages to him in his songs. He said he needed to look in John's eyes and would be arriving shortly.

We didn't know any Claudios and neither did John and Yoko. Everyone thought it was just another crazy and that we shouldn't worry about it. We got a lot of things like that in one form or another every day. There was something about it that made me think that we would hear from Claudio again.

A few days later another telegram from Claudio arrived. We began to take Claudio seriously and we were able to trace the telegram back to a Veterans Administration hospital in the San Francisco area. Apparently Claudio was a shell-shocked Vietnam veteran who was due to be released from the hospital. The consensus was that he would never be able to get over to England and we didn't need to worry. I just didn't feel comfortable with that; something about his telegrams made me feel we would see him.

More telegrams kept coming and then about two weeks later, Les came in to see me and said that there was a scruffy young man waiting out by the gate who insisted that he had come to see John in response to messages that John had sent him. Claudio had arrived.

I went out to talk with him and found a meek, vulnerable young man who obviously was shattered by what he had experienced. He was absolutely convinced that John was sending him messages through his music and that John was asking him to come to see him. I tried to reason with him with statements like: 'John speaks to everyone with his music, Claudio.' Whatever I said didn't work – he knew he was summoned and he said that he would wait. He explained that he needed to look into John's eyes.

Claudio wouldn't leave and the local police wanted to arrest him. John would have none of that. He didn't want him hurt in any way. The police took Claudio into London, but we knew we would see him again and, sure enough, a day later he was back.

John really didn't want the police to arrest him; he was really concerned that he would be hurt more if they did. We had a dilemma. Suddenly I had an idea. 'Why don't you just let him meet you and look into your eyes? We've got lots of people here to protect you. He said that's all he wants and maybe that would work and he would leave,' I said to John.

John was pretty nervous about the idea, but we convinced him that he would be safe. We had plenty of people there since we were still filming *Imagine*. It would be no problem keeping Claudio under control if things went wrong. If we weren't going to have

Claudio arrested, we had to do something. As John started to warm to the idea, he and Yoko sensed that this was a great opportunity to also create a great and potentially meaningful scene for *Imagine*.

'Let's film it,' he said.

We brought Claudio up the drive to the front door. As the cameras rolled, John and Yoko came out to meet him. He stood there in a ratty sheepskin coat; his clothes dirty with his stringy hair hanging down on either side of his face. I didn't know who were more nervous, Claudio or John and Yoko.

John asked Claudio what he wanted. Claudio, obviously stunned to be at last in front of John, murmured that John was sending him messages through his music.

'Don't confuse the songs with your own life . . . I'm just a guy who writes songs,' John said.

'You weren't thinking of anyone in particular when you were singing those . . . ?' murmured Claudio.

This was one of the re-occurring themes of John's life. He wrote for himself from his own feelings and experiences, yet so many people felt that he was writing for them. He was a lodestone that drew people to him; they felt that he had brought some special meaning into their lives.

'I was thinking of me, or at best Yoko, if it was a love song.'

Claudio was still confused.

John could see that Claudio looked pretty frail.

'Ya hungry?' asked John. 'Let's get him something to eat,' he said, looking at us.

We brought him into the kitchen for something to eat. We all settled down at the big kitchen table and as we all ate, the cameras kept rolling.

We never saw Claudio again.

A Custody Trial in St Thomas

When we were travelling, dope was always a problem. Even with the joint-in-the-sink trick, you always ran the risk of being busted just for carrying the pot. I tried to devise a better way to get high without the potential exposure. It was important to keep the risk of a bust to an absolute minimum since John and Yoko were trying to get custody of Kyoko and to get John into the States. I worked out a simple trick inspired by Alice B. Toklas and Gertrude Stein. In her cookbook, Alice Toklas has a recipe for hashish fudge. I asked Ursula Stone, who was working as our au pair looking after Sacha, to make us some brownies. Before they were baked, I dumped in a liberal quantity of some wicked Nigerian grass. When they cooled, I cut them into dainty bite-sized brownies. I then took a posh pastry box from the bakery in Ascot. Lining it with a fancy doily, I filled it with the doped brownies and then closed it and put a decorative bow on it. Lovely!

It was July 21, 1971 and we were flying to Antigua in an attempt to reach Saint Thomas in the Virgin Islands. Another custody hearing for Kyoko was scheduled to be held there. The Virgin Islands were US territory and John couldn't get a visa for the US, but he was not going to let Yoko go alone. We hoped to work something out in Antigua, which was British.

'Dan, let's have a taste of those brownies,' John said, as we settled into our first-class seats. The problem was that the brownies were so good that, because of the grass in them, the more you ate the better they tasted. The box that was meant to last for the whole trip was empty by the time we arrived in Antigua, and we were ridiculously stoned.

'Oh shit,' I muttered to myself, 'I hope the crowd at the airport doesn't recognise John and Yoko.'

In Antigua, I found a pilot with a little Norman Islander like the one we had flown to Spain in. He agreed to take us as long as we paid for both ways in advance in cash, just in case US Immigration wouldn't let John enter at St Thomas.

Harold Seider, Allen Klein's in-house attorney, was in St Thomas already and would be waiting for us at the airport. The way I remember it I called the rock radio station in St Thomas and told them to let everyone know that John was coming in. That should make it more difficult for the US immigration people to turn him away. From the air, we could see the crowds at the airport. With all the publicity and Harold working to pull strings, they let John in on a 24-hour emergency visa.

Harold had arranged for a lovely condo by the sea outside of the capital, Charlotte Amelie. Its white stucco walls shimmered in the sun under aptly-named flamboyant trees aflame with red blossoms. While we waited for the custody hearing, we swam, snorkelled, and found a friendly fellow with a dive boat and some grass he had smuggled in inside an air tank.

One evening in Charlotte Amelie, we entered a restaurant where a band was playing. When they saw John they stopped immediately and began to play *Yesterday*. John was furious that people kept associating him with Paul's song.

The hearing was uneventful. Tony had disappeared with Kyoko again and the court awarded Yoko custody. It was a hollow victory for Yoko who still couldn't see Kyoko. She suspected that Tony had gone to the States and was determined to find him.

With John in possession of his emergency visa, we headed for New York where George Harrison was putting together the 'Concert for Bangladesh' to raise funds for the terrible famine there. We had to pass through the St Juan airport in Puerto Rico and go through US Immigration and Customs again. We were taken aside and interviewed by the US immigration authorities. John and Yoko were taken into another room for almost forty-five minutes. On arriving in New York, Yoko found that her grand-mother's jewellery was missing from her bags.

The Concert for Bangladesh

Tired and frustrated from our trip to St Thomas we settled into the Park Lane Hotel on Central Park South in New York. Tony was now in the States and Yoko's struggle to see Kyoko was shifting there. Yoko and John needed to be in the States now and John's immigration problems were making it extremely difficult to do that. Overstaying a 24-hour emergency visa was not going to work except as a temporary measure. The pressure on them was compounded by George Harrison's impending event on August 1st 1971 at Madison Square Garden, *The Concert For Bangladesh*. It was the first charity event of this kind and the buzz was all over town. Scheduled to appear were George, Bob Dylan, Eric Clapton, Billy Preston, Ravi Shankar, Leon Russell, and many others. As soon as we arrived in New York everyone assumed John would join George and Ringo on stage. John decided not to go on stage for fear of being tricked into a Beatle reunion.

Yoko for her part wanted them to take part. Their careers as rock stars were on different tracks. Yoko was trying to build up her rock chops and wanted to be on stage with George, Ringo, Bob, and Eric. They bickered all day about it

My phone rang in the middle of the night.

'Hello.' I muttered into the phone.

'Get over here right away.'

It was John and from the tone of his voice I could tell that something was wrong. I hurriedly dressed and went down the hall to their suite.

John answered the door and I could see that the room was a mess. Furniture was overturned and things were thrown about. John was very angry and Yoko was huddling in the background.

'What happened?' I asked.

'I'm leaving. Help me get out to the airport,' said John.

'What about Yoko?'

'She wants to stay. I'm leaving, let's go.'

I was not going anywhere until I knew Yoko was all right. He wanted to go immediately, but I persuaded him to wait while I called for some discreet help to come and be with Yoko and get the room straightened out. I started to call a limo but John just wanted to go. He was too angry to return to Ascot so he told me he was going to get a cab to the airport and fly to Paris immediately. I knew he liked Paris and he could go there and still be close to Ascot.

'John, it's going to look bad if the press learns that you and Yoko are on different continents. Are you really sure you want to leave?'

'She wants to go on-stage at George's Bangladesh thing. I'm not gonna do it. If she wants to go on without me, let her. I'll be in Paris.'

He was adamant and obviously very upset and angry. I just couldn't persuade him to reconsider, so I called May Pang to come over to take care of Yoko, and John and I went down to the lobby and caught a cab to JFK. We rode out to the airport in a terrible rainstorm. John's stared grimly ahead as we ploughed through the deluge. I got him on a flight to Paris and returned to the Park Lane and Yoko.

I got back by mid-morning and May had cleaned up the room and Yoko was looking a lot better. Very hurt and upset over the fight with John, she told me that she was going to go on-stage without him. I couldn't talk her out of it. We went over to Allen Klein's office, and no matter what Allen and I said, she still insisted that she was going to go on.

We told her that it could destroy John and Yoko in the public eye. We pointed out that George and Ringo would be extremely uncomfortable with it, but she didn't care; she was going onto that stage and she was going to sing. We talked to and cajoled her throughout the day and finally she relented. We returned to the Park Lane to pack and then caught a flight that night to London. She was on her way to Ascot and John was in Paris. The press hadn't found out that anything was going on, but they were still apart.

The next day a contrite John, preceded by a lot of flowers, turned up at Ascot.

Less than two weeks later John and Yoko left for New York, and although they couldn't have known it at the time, they would never return to Tittenhurst again.

The Ascot period was a necessary transition for all of us. I had broken my dependence on heroin and started on the road to recovery. Yoko had established herself as more that just the woman who had 'broken up the Beatles'. John had changed from a Beatle to the John Lennon that we know today. From the time he met Yoko he went through a rapid period of growth both as a person and an artist. To develop the ideas and use the new freedom Yoko had introduced him to, he had to free himself from Apple and the Beatles and he needed a refuge like Tittenhurst. It was an incubator where they could work together developing ideas and projects while protected from the world. One can clearly see the evolution his work went through starting with the conceptualist collaborations of their first art albums and films, through the break-out matching Plastic Ono albums, to John's fully realised solo work *Imagine*. When John and Yoko moved into Tittenhurst in August of 1969 he was still a Beatle and a tentative neophyte in Yoko's conceptualist world. When he left for New York almost exactly two years later with the master tape for *Imagine*, he had completed his transformation. He had discovered his new voice and he had a confidence that would stay with him for the rest of his life. Tittenhurst had served its purpose and he was ready to leave. New York was where the energy was and he was ready to take it on. He had assimilated Yoko's gift and it was this new John Lennon who would have such a profound effect on the world.

Some Time in New York City

Ascot became like a ghost town after John and Yoko left for New York. All the energy that surrounded them, the vortex, and the focus shifted and suddenly an eerie quiet descended on the place. We still had piles of work to do, so many films, recordings and projects had been produced in the Ascot cauldron that had to be managed and there really wasn't a system to do it in New York. But without John and Yoko around the magic and energy was gone. The parade had gone by and a quiet descended. John and Yoko's wing of the building was empty and the studio silent.

Something insidious was happening to me. When an addict stops one form of poison the addiction is replaced or pops up in another form. I had been riding on the whirlwind of being around John and Yoko all the time. The electricity that surrounded them had become my substitute for the heroin high and now I was left with my buzzless boring methadone.

I hadn't really cured myself of the opiate addiction. I had stopped injecting heroin on a daily basis, but I had traded it for Methadone. Methadone is a strange drug. It was rumoured that it had been developed by Hitler prior to the war, because Germany didn't have access to the opium fields in the south. You take it by mouth and you get calm, but you don't get high. There is no rush, no thrill like heroin. It comes on slowly, it stays with you for a very long time and it leaves slowly. There is no frenetic up and down that you get with Horse. You take heroin and you get high immediately, you get the rush that the junkies come to crave, you're high for a bit, and then after a few hours you start to come down and you're sick again so you need more. Methadone gets rid of all of this because it is so slow acting and there is no appreciable high with it. That's

184

why it's used as a substitute for heroin. The real issue is that you are still addicted to an opiate and it can still damage you in the long term just like heroin and morphine and the other more recreational versions of the opiates. You haven't dealt with the problems of addiction itself. You've simply swept them under the carpet, you're still an addict. You've traded a messy, scary, exciting, violent, terrifying addiction for a long heavy, boring one.

As I moved into the fall of 1971 the glamour of being John and Yoko's guy was beginning to wear a little thin. With them in New York, things began to change. They had decided to stay there until John could travel in and out of the States freely. I found myself looking after an empty Ascot and working on getting all the films organised and distributed. This was difficult as the films were considered art films and distributors were not very interested in them. Using John and Yoko's name I could get meetings, but my efforts were producing little results. Aside from the day-to-day obligations, all the film work was taking a lot of my time.

Jill was pregnant and the baby was due in October. I was determined not to leave Ascot until the baby arrived. John and Yoko always had emergencies that had to be attended to. Yoko called with things that needed my attention, but I was adamant about staying with Jill. I was tired of being around them every day, making sure that every whim was taken care of, while at the same time having to handle more and more of the administrative side of their projects and affairs. My new baby came first.

John and Yoko set up operations in a large cluster of suites in the St Regis Hotel across from Central Park on Fifth Avenue. They had an editing room set up. Steve Gebhardt, Bob Fries, and Doug Ibold were shooting and cutting together more footage for *Imagine*, which was growing quickly into a full-length film. I got daily reports of their antics. There was a constant flow of people through the suite. When John heard that someone like Fred Astaire or Jack Palance was in the hotel, he would ring them up and invite them by and they would become part of *Imagine*. When I heard they were filming Fred Astaire, I really wished I was there. Being a mime and choreographer, he had always been one of my heroes.

John and Yoko were really committed to staying in New York. Joe Butler, of the band the Loving Spoonful, rented them his basement apartment in the West Village on Bank Street. Yoko bought a small loft building on Broome Street, just off West Broadway. Their film operations, Joko Films, could operate out of the Broome Street building and John and Yoko moved into the tiny apartment. Bob Fries secured a space to use as a recording studio on 10th Street just a few blocks from the Bank Street apartment. They were ready to settle in as New Yorkers.

On October 25, 1971, in Queen Charlotte's Nursing Home in Windsor, Jill gave birth to a beautiful boy. Looking at him, we decided he resembled my father so we named him Mischa after him. Looking at little Mischa in my arms I decided that the time had come for the next step in my career. I was stronger now and confident that I could begin to deal with the outside world again. I didn't know yet what I was going to do, but I knew it had something to do with film. I began to make plans.

Near the end of November, with Mischa and Jill doing well, I went to New York. I wasn't prepared for how much John and Yoko had changed. To start with, I was stunned by the Bank Street apartment. It was tiny! You walked down some steps from the street to a small door that opened onto a little room. It had low ceilings, and was narrow and dark. In the front, there was a small desk set up by a dingy window that looked out to the street above. The end of the room had what appeared to be the smallest kitchen I had ever seen. I walked through a door at the back that opened onto a big atelier with skylights. John and Yoko were up on a big bed with a large Sony TV and telephones.

'Hi Dan, how's the baby?' John asked.

'Great. He's beautiful and Jill is doing fine. She sends her love.'

Over the next few days the picture of their new life in New York unfolded. Sitting on the bed, they smoked dope, watched TV, and took their methadone. It was here that they held court to Black Panthers, various hippie radicals, underground artists, and sycophant celebrities. Jerry Rubin, one of the 'Chicago Eight', who had been accused of conspiracy and incitement to riot during the 1968 Democratic Convention, was often up on the bed with them, basking in their presence.

Peter Bendrey had come out from Ascot to look after their day-to-day needs. Peter, more at home in India with a sitar, was uncomfortable in a tiny New York pad.

I liked Broome Street a lot more. Steve, Bob, and Doug had set up a group of elegant KEM editing tables on the second floor and Doug was sleeping there.

I was suspicious of the whole setup at Bank Street. The security sucked. All the hangers-on were there to be around John and to use his star status to promote their own agendas. I sometimes thought that Yoko created these situations. I could hear her saying, 'Let's live in a little apartment in the Village. We can really be in touch . . . '

Yoko must have been aware of how dangerous it was becoming. She was obviously very nervous and had developed the habit of constantly cutting her nails as she sat there in a dope haze. John and his sycophants discussed how they were going to disrupt the Democratic Convention in Miami, as Yoko looked for another bit of nail to trim from her fingers.

Tom Basalari, their limo driver, brought back prescriptions for Methadone from a doctor in Queens.

John and Yoko's idealism had changed in the political pressure cooker of New York. There had always been a hard side to John's politics rooted in his lower class Liverpool background. Sometimes you sensed a deep anger when he talked. It was masked by his intelligence and humour, but it was there. It was a kind of working-class anger at the authority that had always used and abused them. There in New York of November 1971, hanging out with underground activists, with the world exploding, who knew what would happen next.

Peter slept on a small cramped bed in the front room. He was great; he would follow them into hell, rolling them another joint and cooking macrobiotic food. He was too young and too nice. He lived at Bank Street around the clock, keeping them supplied with grass, tea, and Cokes. Dr Pepper seemed to have been just a passing fad.

The politicisation of John and Yoko was complete. Their days spent with Jerry Rubin in bed beside them, smoking dope and planning the downfall of Nixon and the end of the Vietnam War, led to a plan to do a series of concerts leading up to the Republican Convention the following August in San Diego. The forthcoming election would be the first in which eighteen-year-olds could vote. Jerry and the rest of the politicos figured John would be perfect as he could deliver the young. They would come to see him and leave ready to demonstrate and vote. If Nixon and the Republicans thought the melee at the Democratic Convention in '68 was bad, Jerry argued, wait till they saw the results of the planned concert tour ending in San Diego.

John had a knack for rubbing authority figures the wrong way and what greater authority figure than Richard Nixon, president of the United States? John was not physically brave, but he was drawn again and again to this kind of controversy. When he was younger and drank too much, he used to fight, but the John I knew was cautious and sometimes almost effeminate. I wondered if he understood how serious things were about to become. The truth was that I was scared for us all.

I used to sit in front of the little window that looked out at Bank Street where we had a desk and a phone. To get into the apartment, you descended a few steps from the street to the little door with garbage cans beside it. The window was dirty with the grime of the city and looked up to the street. You saw the legs of passers-by. On the street in front, I saw a fellow working on a motorcycle a few feet from the door.

'I bet he is a FBI agent,' said Peter in his soft, tentative voice as he looked over my shoulder.

'Why do you say that? He just looks like a dude working on his bike.'

'Hey man, he works on it all day long, every day.'

'That could be a problem.' I felt a cold chill in my stomach.

'I'm sure he's a FBI agent. He takes that bike apart and then puts it back together over and over,' said Peter.

I stayed in a room at the nearby 5th Avenue Hotel when I was in town. I mulled over the horrendous security problems. Bank Street reeked of paranoia. John and Yoko were sure the FBI was taping their calls. I bought a tiny voice-activated Nagra tape recorder to put on the telephone so we could record all their calls. I figured if Nixon had his goons taping them, they could be edited to make them more damning than they really were. With the tapes we made we could prove what was really said. Even though John was deep into the radical movement at that point he wasn't violent or reckless.

Things weren't all bad. There was time for John and I to have our clothing exchanges.

'Where did you get that shirt, Dan?' John was looking at a Wrangler cowboy shirt I was wearing.

'At the Wrangler shop on Greenwich Avenue . . . nothing fancy, just standard cowboy issue.'

'It really looks great, man.'

'I'll pick you up a few.'

Some good news was that John was beginning to mellow toward Paul McCartney. John agreed to talk to him on the telephone. We had found out how to reach him where he was performing. After talking to a number of his people, I finally got Paul on the phone and John took the call. We all hoped this was the beginning of reconciliation between the two of them.

Ten for Two and *Attica* at the Apollo

On Friday, December 10, 1971 John and Yoko went to Ann Arbor Michigan, for what was billed as the *Ten for Two* concert. John Sinclair, a radical leader, music guru, and member of the White Panthers had been arrested in Michigan and sentenced to ten years in jail for two marijuana joints. The White Panthers were known for the slogan, 'Everything free for everybody!' The ground swell of support for Sinclair among the counterculture was reaching its culmination. A free concert had been planned at the University of Michigan Chrysler Basketball arena in Ann Arbor and John and Yoko were going.

In preparation for the concert, Bank Street was a flurry of activity. All around John and Yoko's bed, members of the counterculture made plans. As John and Yoko's involvement with the Yippies grew, Jerry Rubin grew in stature and was seen beside them on the big bed more than ever. John had written a song for the event and he planned to twang 'It ain't fair, John Sinclair in the stir for breathing air' on his new National steel guitar. Bobby Seale of the Black Panthers was going to speak. So were Jerry, Allen Ginsberg, and Rennie Davis, one of the Chicago Eight. Stevie Wonder and Bob Seger had agreed to sing.

David Peel, a wild counterculture singer who often performed in Washington Square, planned to sing his song *The Pope Smokes Dope* and play with John and Yoko.

While John co-ordinated the music and Jerry the political side of things, I hustled to arrange some kind of security for the event. John and Yoko decided to make a film of the event so Steve Gebhardt and Bob Fries rushed to put together a crew. The *Ten for Two Concert* would give them a chance to once again use the multi-camera and microphone techniques they were perfecting to shoot concerts. Joko Films was getting busier and busier.

The biggest problem in making a documentary of a rock and roll concert was that it was very hard to hear anything using traditional documentary techniques. The Maysles Brothers had shot the Beatles at Shea Stadium and the sound track was almost unusable. Rock and roll audiences were noisy and Beatles audiences roared deafeningly from the moment the musicians came on stage. When D.A. Pennebaker screened his footage from the Toronto Rock and Roll Revival for us, the sound track was just too noisy.

Bob Fries had put together a recording truck with a console and multi-track tape recorders. The truck would drive to a concert venue and then Bob would mike each of the performers and their instruments. By having a directional mike for each of them separate from the PA system, Bob could feed each mike back to its own discrete track on the tape machine. He recorded each voice and instrument separated from the overall roar of the concert. He then synced all the cameras up to the recording so that if John was singing, every camera would film his lips moving in time to the music.

Steve was wrangling together multiple cameras to film the Ann Arbor concert. Since each camera could be synced up to recording tracks, we could use as many cameras as we needed and the budget would allow. Steve would be on stage with a hand-held camera, wearing a headset so that he could communicate to the other cameramen and Bob, who would be on one of the cameras or in the recording truck. When it all came back to Broome Street, we could use the array of KEM three-screen editing decks to see all the pieces together.

'Can you see anything in my ear?' Jerry Rubin asked me.

We had all converged on Ann Arbor and settled into hotels and motels around the University of Michigan campus. I was in a room with Jerry, who was very nervous. For hours, he was trying on different shirts and saying, 'Do I look all right?' Finally, he settled down but in the middle of the night he woke up with a terrible earache and I had to get him a doctor who fixed him up enough so that he was ready to go on stage.

My main concerns were logistics and security. Chrysler was a large basketball arena and the stage was surrounded by people on all sides. Everyone would be smoking dope and we had a collection of the most politically and socially radical firebrands of the day. We were one step removed from the Weather Underground. My biggest concern after John and Yoko's safety was Bobby Seale. His people would not agree to anything. 'Just tell us when Bobby's supposed to speak and we'll take care of everything,' they said.

The event started at about four in the afternoon and progressed with speakers and music all through the afternoon and into the evening. As the speakers and acts were doing their thing, poor Steve and Bob lugged the cameras from shot to shot. Steve carried a hand-held Arriflex BL camera supported against his large frame by a body brace all day and into the night.

Jerry Rubin and Rennie Davis gave speeches. Stevie Wonder, Phil Ochs, Bob Seger, Commander Cody, and other musicians sang for the crowd. Allen Ginsberg harangued everyone with poetry. When it came time for Black Panther Chairman Bobby Seale to speak, a group of young Panthers making up Bobby's security detail solemnly marched into the auditorium. They looked very serious in their black leather jackets and black berets. When they reached the stage, they make a tight circle around it facing out toward the audience. They also lined the way in. Once they were in position, Bobby came out and delivered a fiery speech.

It was after one in the morning when John and Yoko finally came on stage. They looked harried and tired. I watched them with mixed emotions. It made me very nervous to see them surrounded by so many people in such a chaotic situation, but at the same time, there was something very noble about a star of John's calibre singing here at the very centre of the movement to stop the war. He was at his most political, singing *Attica State*, about the massacre at Attica State prison in New York. He also sang *Luck of the Irish* about the troubles in Northern Ireland. Yoko sang *Sisters, Oh Sisters*. They ended their performance with John's song, *John Sinclair*, accompanied by David Peel.

The law in Michigan had already been changed before the concert. *Ten for Two* brought a lot of publicity and John Sinclair was released three days later.

'It's very cool, man. We are going up to the Apollo Theatre for the Attica benefit.'

John was explaining their plans to participate in a benefit for the Attica prisoners at the Apollo Theatre in Harlem on December He was both nervous and excited about going uptown. The Apollo was a legendary centre of black culture on 125th street right in the middle of Harlem It was opened in 1914 as a burlesque theatre, and renamed in 1934. Since then, it played a key role in the careers of a never-ending parade of show business legends, including Sarah Vaughan and Ella Fitzgerald.

To provide security, Bobby Seale sent a contingent of young Panthers to guard John and Yoko. They arrived at the door of Bank Street dressed in black leather jackets and black berets.

'I bet they're armed,' I muttered to Peter as they waited for John and Yoko to come out.

As the caravan of limos left for the Apollo, I went over to our suspected FBI guy out front who was still repairing his motorcycle.

'They're going up to the Apollo Theatre for the Attica benefit and will be coming back or going to Jerry Rubin's after. I hope we can avoid any trouble.'

'I don't know what you're talking about,' he replied.

To avoid the crowds when we arrived at the Apollo, we pulled the limo into an alley by the stage door at the rear of the theatre. I stayed outside to speak to Tom, the limo driver. As Tom drove away, I tried the stage door but it must have locked automatically when it closed.

'Oh shit,' I thought. 'It's night time and I'm a white beatnik standing alone in an alley in Harlem.'

I banged on the door and after what seemed like an eternity it opened. I slid in to a very dark and cramped backstage area jammed full of all kinds of folks. So many great artists had performed here. This was where a fifteen-year-old Ella Fitzgerald had won the talent contest on the first amateur night held there.

I climbed up a narrow flight of stairs and found John and Yoko in a tiny dressing room with the young Panthers diligently guarding the door. As I squeezed in, John introduced me to Aretha Franklin. Her son, a handsome young man in uniform with medals on his chest, was with her. He was serving in Vietnam and quite a contrast to the rest of the furry antiwar radicals surrounding John and Yoko.

When John went on stage the crowd exploded. He sang the song he had written for the event, *Attica State*. He explained to the audience that since he had lost his old band, he was busking it. Then he went into *Imagine*.

On Christmas Eve, I returned to Jill, Sacha, and Mischa and the peace of Ascot. I was worn out from all the events and politics,

In the twelve-step programmes the first step we take is to acknowledge that we are powerless over alcohol and drugs. The second step is to realise that a power greater than ourselves can restore us to sanity. I knew I had been powerless over heroin but I thought that giving it up and going through prolonged withdrawal was all I needed to do. I didn't think of myself as an addict and alcoholic, and I didn't even consider a power greater than myself or that I needed to be restored to sanity. I had been filling the emptiness I felt after heroin with pot and booze. I never let myself get completely out of it. I drank sparingly; I didn't like being out of control. Like many addicts and alcoholics I was still using substances to cover my feelings. What I didn't know then that I know now is that an addict will always be an addict whether he is using or not. But with the heroin no longer going into my arm I wanted to get back on track and I was determined to do it.

Changes

Back in the sixties we always talked about 'changes' or 'the changes'. We felt that when we had expanded our consciousness with drugs we became more sensitive to the subtle changes and nuances in our environment. The first half of 1972 was a time of change. I found myself travelling constantly between New York and London and I was spending more and more time trying to get John and Yoko's films distributed. During January I set up an office at Apple on St James just off Piccadilly. I had an all black screening room with a conference table and a row of first-class aeroplane seats. Next to it was a fully equipped editing room and a full-time editor named Carmac. We provided him with a multi-head Kem editing table like the ones we were using at Broome Street.

My efforts to stay off heroin were being undermined. I was still keeping away from it, but life at the Apple office was exposing me to a ready supply of cocaine. I always identified cocaine with the period when I was a registered addict. Using it brought back some of those old feelings and associations. The fact that I had never stopped using marijuana and alcohol had kept me in a vulnerable state. We addicts and alcoholics have a hard time staying off one addictive substance if we go on using another. You have to smother the disease completely if you want to stay clean. But I didn't know that then, and even if I had known, I wonder if I would have really believed it. Denial in an addict is a powerful thing and until we are really ready, we justify switching from one poison to another.

Ringo also had offices at Apple. He was recording, acting in films, and had started a high-end furniture company. I was getting sucked into the decadence of the period. A typical day might include Cuban cigars from Mayfair, oysters for lunch at Pruniers, and a touch of coke. The coke seemed a natural part of the life I was living. I regularly relaxed with Ringo's financial guy, Hilary Gerrard and Neil Aspinall. He always seemed to have lines of coke laid out on the glass coffee table in Ringo's office. Ringo was, as always, amiable and easy-going, but he was increasingly concerned by all the money Apple was spending on John and Yoko's film projects.

John wanted to get the film of *Imagine* into distribution. It was more than an art film and while it lacked a story arc, it was long enough for theatrical distribution. He asked me to show it to Sir Lew Grade who ran ITV and had bought a big hunk of the Beatles Northern Songs. I called Sir Lew, told him John wanted his help with *Imagine*, and sent him a print.

A few days later, I visited him at his office near Marble Arch. He was sitting behind a large desk with a panorama of London spread out in the big window behind him.

'Come on in,' he said. 'I'd do anything for the boys. How is John, anyway?'

He was smoking a gigantic cigar. Lew and his brothers, Bernard and Leslie, had been major forces in the British entertainment industry for years. They had come to the UK from the Ukraine in 1912. Looking at him, it was hard to imagine that he had been the world Charleston champion in 1926.

Sir Lew was very kind, but he passed on the project, saying that there was nothing he could do with *Imagine*.

We would have to focus on independent distribution opportunities.

Meanwhile in February, back in the States, Nixon began to fight back and the Feds served John with a deportation order. He was given sixty days to leave the country. The basis for the order was his phony conviction in London for possession of cannabis. The implications for Yoko's search for Kyoko were dire, since Tony could now continue hiding her in the States. If John was deported, Yoko would not be able to continue her search.

All of a sudden, the idea of the concert tour leading up to the Republican Convention was abandoned and John and Yoko found themselves in a desperate fight to remain in the States.

At the same time, I had also come under attack. Jill, a British citizen, was denied a visa to travel to the States on the grounds of my past involvement with drugs.

John and Yoko hired Leon Wildes, a top immigration attorney, to represent them. Leon was a sweet and brilliant man. He was charmingly formal, soft-spoken, and deliberate. John and Yoko encouraged us to use him for Jill's case as well.

Tony resurfaced in Houston with Kyoko and his new companion Melinda. Proceedings were starting there for Yoko to get custody of Kyoko. We received information that Tony and Melinda were involved in a Jesus freak commune.

John, Yoko, and I flew to Houston to meet with local attorneys. On the way down John said he was thinking of writing a country song about Yoko trying to find Kyoko. It might persuade people to help them with Yoko's struggle to see her daughter.

On the deportation front John and Yoko had begun a campaign to fight back. John had started to wear suits and they continued to talk in earnest to the press and TV about their plight and concerns for Kyoko.

Michael X – The Murders in Trinidad

It was May of 1972 and the changes were getting weirder. It was one of those beautiful spring days we get in England, but I was aware that things were changing.

'Dan, look at the paper.' Jill handed me the afternoon newspaper that had just arrived. 'Michael's been arrested in Trinidad.' Michael X, who had left England for Trinidad, was in trouble again.

Looking at the paper, I saw a picture of Michael being arrested. Three bodies had been dug up at Michael's place in Trinidad. He had been charged with the murders.

The telephone began to ring. First I got a call from Alex Trocchi, who had just read the article. We talked about what to do. Alex had tried to phone Trinidad, but was unable to reach anyone.

Then John and Yoko phoned wanting to know what was happening.

'I don't know yet, I just saw it in the news. I'll call you as soon as I have any information.'

They were genuinely concerned about Michael, and needed as much information as they could get. People would start asking their opinion about Michael's case and the events in Trinidad.

The next day, the papers carried photos of our friends Granger and Trina who had just returned from Trinidad. They were at Michael's place when the bodies were found and apparently when the murders took place.

I went into town to meet them at Alex's. They were both tall and lanky with unruly blond hair. I knew them from my heroin days. Alex was at the centre of what was going on in London among Michael's artist friends and as we talked the telephone kept ringing.

'It was crazy. He wasn't even there,' said Granger. 'He was down

in Guyana for an Independence Day celebration, giving a speech.'
Granger was pretty shaken up, having just gone through a rough
two or three days.

'Did you guys see or hear anything?' I asked.

'No, man, everything was laid back. Sure, there were these Black
Muslim guys, but nobody was uptight or angry. We were as
surprised as anyone when they dug up the bodies.'

The whole thing was creepy and being at Alex's scared me – I
couldn't stop thinking about heroin. On top of that, Michael's
situation seemed fishy. He had fallen out with Elijah Muhammad,
the head of the Black Muslims in the States. Two of the bodies
were local gardeners and one was Gale Benson, the daughter of a
Conservative MP. Gale had been living with a Black Muslim
named Hakim Jamal. We all thought it was some kind of set up. It
seemed to be the only logical explanation. Michael had become a
thorn in the side of Elijah Muhammad. Like Malcolm X before
him, he had broken away from the rigid control of Elijah
Muhammad and had developed a following separate from the
mainstream Black Muslims in the US.

Michael's wife Desirée was still in the UK. John, Yoko, and I
helped form the Committee to Support Michael X. John and
Yoko had contacted the radical attorneys William Kunstler and
Margie Rattner, both of whom came to England.

'So that was the basis for your performance in *2001*?' Asked Bill
Kunstler, as we looked at Guy the gorilla at the London Zoo. Guy
was massive and he looked back at us morosely. I had used Guy as
a model for my character in *2001*.

Bill, Margie, Jill, and I were taking a walk through the Zoo trying
to develop a strategy. A few days later, I joined the attorneys and
Alex Trocchi at a press conference announcing the formation of
the Committee. The writer Kate Millett and a number of other
literary and celebrity types joined us on the committee.

Bill Kunstler went to visit Michael and decided he had to track down Gale Benson's boyfriend, Hakim Jamal. Bill found out he was in Boston. Everyone felt that Hakim knew the truth about what had happened and Bill was going up to interview him. The day before he left, Hakim answered his door and a couple of guys in black suits and shades pulled out guns and blew him away. That was really Michael's last chance. Bill visited him a number of times and told us he was in a subterranean cell like something from a horror movie. He had to bend down to speak to him through a low barred window.

The pressure around me in London was immense. I felt like a squirrel on a wheel in a cage, endlessly running. The combination of the cocaine and trying to stay on top of all the rock and roll craziness was pushing me closer and closer to a fix. On May 16th, 1975 Michael was hanged. The night before, Michael sent me a very moving letter in which he asked me to help with his papers and make sure Desirée was looked after.

Cannes, Ringo, and George

I kept trying to get a distribution deal put together for *Imagine*. You'd think selling a John Lennon film would be like shooting fish in a barrel. *Imagine* was considered a little too short for feature distribution; also, general audiences regarded John and Yoko's film projects as experimental counter-cultural work. There was always an inherent conflict in what they did. The techniques of conceptual art that Yoko had brought to their films didn't lend themselves to the tastes of the mass markets. Yoko's films were art films without the story and character development of most popular films. I discussed the films with Andy Warhol's distributor, Jimmy Vaughan of Vaughan Films. Jimmy was interested, but he could only get limited art-house bookings for them.

John and Yoko still wanted mainstream distribution, so I rented a theatre for a week at the Cannes Film Festival during May of 1972. They asked me to check with Ringo and George to see if they had anything to show. Apple was footing all the bills for John and Yoko's film activities, so it was natural to include George and Ringo in the screenings. Ringo had played a role in a spaghetti western called *Blindman*, directed by Ferdinando Baldi, and starring Tony Anthony.

George had appeared in a beautiful documentary called *Raga* about Ravi Shankar and his music. It was written by Nancy Bacal, Michael X's girlfriend, and directed by Howard Worth. I was glad to have the opportunity to screen it.

Along with *Imagine*, *Raga*, and *Blindman*, I had *El Topo*, a cult hit John and Yoko had bought. *El Topo* was a disturbing surrealist picture made in Mexico by Alejandro Jodorowsky.

We set up operations, armed with T-shirts and collateral materials, and rented Cinema La Star right in the centre of Cannes for two hours each night at the same time. I hired Richard Dembo to be our publicist and help us facilitate all the showings.

I was approached immediately by distributors wanting to buy *El Topo*. I called John and Yoko and they assured me that they didn't want to sell. I think they were peeved that it was getting much more attention than their films. Every time someone made me an offer and I turned it down, they came back with a higher one. Distributors were stopping me on the street.

Once we actually screened *El Topo*, the bidding really escalated. It got so ridiculous that I called John and Yoko again.

'John, this is crazy. We can make a lot of money if we cut a deal.'

'OK, call Allen.'

I called Allen Klein. When he heard how high the offers were, he decided to fly in Peter Howard from the Apple office in London to see if a deal could be made.

Ringo and George had arrived for their screenings. The highlight of the week was a dinner on a humongous yacht Ringo had rented. It took place in the yacht's dining room which was covered with silk chinoiserie wallpaper. While waiters served our meal, Ringo held court, urbane and cheerful as always.

I was sitting beside George, who was his usual taciturn and mildly humorous self.

'Do you have a doogie?' he whispered to me, using the slang for a marijuana joint. He seemed a bit bored.

'Yeah, do you want to do it?'

We slipped away from the table and made our way up to the top deck where we found a place to sit in the moonlight. We could see the lights of the boats and the shore beyond.

'That's a pretty fancy dinner Ringo has going down there,' he said.

'Yeah, it's nice to take a break.'

It was a really peaceful night away from the hullabaloo and madness of Cannes. Talking quietly, surrounded by the shelter of darkness, we smoked the joint.

Ladies and Gentlemen, the Rolling Stones

I was spending a lot of time in England, working out of my office and editing room at Apple. John and Yoko were working on a major show of Yoko's artwork at the Everson Museum in Rochester, New York. John was making some of the pieces for the show.

Sometime in July, Steve Gebhardt called me from the States in the middle of the night.

'Robert Frank, Danny Seymour, and some of the guys from Atlantic Records want us to film the Stones. They need concert footage to go with a documentary Robert and Danny shot of their tour.'

'Who is we?' I was pissed at being woken up at three in the morning.

'Fries and me, we talked with them about four concerts this weekend in Texas.'

'How do John and Yoko feel about that?' I mumble.

'I haven't told them – that's why I'm calling you,' Steve answered.

'Don't worry, I'll take care of it. Make sure we pay for the negative.' I rolled over and went back to sleep.

Steve and Bob filmed the Stones concerts and returned to New York with thousands of feet of film. It was great footage and we realised it could stand on its own as a film or TV show. They had used multiple cameras and multi-track recording. It was stylistically very different from Robert and Danny's documentary *Cocksucker Blues*, which followed the off-stage goings on of the tour. It was a hand-held, funky, and very raunchy film.

While John and Yoko agreed that we could do the project, I sensed a tension when we discussed it. Up till then, we had only produced their own films.

Joko Films was growing fast. The building on Broome Street was filled with people working round the clock. Editing the footage for *Imagine* and *Ten for Two* had taken a lot of time and money. With the Stones film in hand, we had to expand. John and Yoko's first films were shorter and made in a hurry with few resources. Shot in sixteen millimeter, we had to blow them up to thirty-five so they could be shown in theatres. Steve Gebhardt spent a lot of time up at EUE Screens Gems in New York, going through the expensive and time-consuming process of making the thirty-five millimeter negatives. Apple was paying all the bills and we weren't making any money. Only art houses and museums were interested in showing their films.

Bob Fries was in London to show clips of four of the songs from the Stones concerts he and Steve had shot in Texas. Keith, Mick, and some of the guys from The Who, went to the screening. After seeing the footage, Mick didn't want to continue with the project as a film. He thought it should be made into a TV show. Keith wanted it to be a movie so he took over.

'Where did they mix *Lawrence of Arabia*?' Keith asked Bob and I. He wanted to do a quadraphonic mix of the songs.

'Twickenham. Yeah, it was Twickenham.' I said.

'Then that's where I'll do the mix,' said Keith.

Keith was a character. He looked like a walking disaster area, but he was smart enough underneath the bad boy veneer and musically very astute.

Mick was totally together. When we met with him in the editing room in my Apple office, I realised I was talking to a very smart businessman – cool, relaxed, and completely different from his public persona except for a provocative bulge in his tight pants.

Bob and I arranged for Keith to work at Twickenham. One of Bob's jobs was to make sure the studio was stocked with Courvoisier and other goodies. Bob came down to my office after visiting with Ringo and Al Steckler. Al had come over from Allen Klein's New

York office where he was in charge of music projects. Ringo's concerns were growing over the money Apple was spending on John's film projects.

'Ringo and Al just put me on the carpet and really grilled me,' said Bob.

'Were they pissed about the Stones?' I asked.

'A bit, but more about the money Joko is spending. They're concerned about Broome Street, all the people working in New York, the labs, everything.'

What made the situation more complicated was that the Stones film was generating more commercial interest that John and Yokos' art films.

The One to One Concerts

During the summer of 1972, Geraldo Rivera, a reporter for WABC-TV in New York gave John and Yoko a lot of TV coverage of their search for Kyoko. In return for the publicity, John and Yoko raised money for Geraldo's Willowbrook Foundation. He had presented a series exposing the deplorable conditions at Willowbrook State School for the Mentally Ill. It had catapulted him into the public eye and led to a government investigation. On August 30th at Madison Square Garden, John and Yoko put on two big concerts called 'One to One'. We planned to film them and made a TV special for ABC.

I found myself trying to manage a zoo of celebrities and film and recording crews. We did one show in the afternoon and another in the evening.

Just getting the shows mounted was a major pain in the ass. Everyone donated their time but the cameramen's local union turned out to be very difficult. Steve and Bob wanted to use their own people, documentary guys who were hip to rock and roll and familiar with the sixteen millimeter Arriflexs we were using. Since the Garden was a union house, the locals wanted us to use guys from their roster. They refused to donate any time to the charity and demanded to be paid for the concert and the TV show, as well as overtime. With a lot of arguing and complaining, we worked things out and by the day of the shows, things were looking good.

We moved the recording truck in backstage and set up camera positions all over the Garden. We were ready to record the first of the two shows that made up the concert.

In the dressing room before the evening show, John's pre-gig jitters were worse than usual. He hadn't played a venue this important in a long time. The ABC television special would be watched by millions of people.

Bob Fries told him they needed to change the balance of sound in the hall.

'I'm the one who has to play in front of all these people. It's your job to take care of the sound system,' John snapped at him.

Turning to me, John said, 'Ask little Stevie Wonder what songs he's going to do. I want to make sure we don't do the same ones.' John referred to Stevie by his old name even though he was not little any more.

'Sure, John.'

John started pacing about and fiddling with his hair. Yoko seemed calm on the surface, but she was nervous, too. I left the dressing room to find Stevie.

He was sitting in his dressing room surrounded by his people. They took me over to him and when I spoke, he reached up and felt for my hand. He wanted to touch me because he couldn't see me.

'Mr Wonder, uh, Stevie, John wants to know what songs you're planning on doing so that he doesn't play the same things.'

As we talked, he moved his head from side to side as if he was scanning me. He told me his play list and I took it back to John.

When I looked in on Geraldo I could see he was anxious. Standing in the middle of his dressing room, he was staring at his shoes with a perplexed look on his face.

'What do you think about my shoes?' he asked. 'I just bought them. Do you think they go with what I'm wearing?'

'The shoes look great, Geraldo – you look great.'

Peeking out at the auditorium, I saw Mayor Lindsay and a number of notables. Geraldo's wife, Edith, was sitting with her father, Kurt Vonnegut. Eleanor McGovern, the wife of the Democratic presidential candidate George McGovern, was out there with friends. Because of all the celebrities, the Garden was crawling with scores of security people. Mrs McGovern was being watched by the Secret Service.

I was trying my best to prevent anyone from getting busted. I had to make sure Phil Spector stayed away from all the security goons, particularly the Secret Service.

'Check out these drapes, man.' It was Stan Bronstein, who played the sax, clarinet, and did vocals for Elephant's Memory, the band John was playing with.

'*Très* cool, man.' I was standing with Stan, admiring the pair of fifties draped pants he had bought for the concert.

'Yeah, I figure I'll outdo the guys from Sha Na Na.'

We both laughed. John had been playing with Elephant's Memory for a while. Stan and drummer Rick Frank founded the band back in 1967 and were best known for the hit song *Old Man Willow* from the soundtrack of *Midnight Cowboy*. Rick's father had been my doctor when I was a kid suffering from migraines.

John had invited Sha Na Na to perform. They dressed and sang like a classic fifties group.

The Garden filled and somehow we got the whole show started. As things began to rock the whole floor of the Stadium moved up and down with the beat.

My first thought was, 'Oh shit, I must be stoned!'

'Can you feel it, man? I think the floor is moving,' I said to Claude Hayn, the Elephants' road manager who was standing beside me.

'Check out the limos, man,' Claude said, pointing to the convoy of black limos parked in a cluster behind the stage. As I looked over at them, I could see they were rocking up and down as the floor moved.

'Fucking-A man, they're rocking to the beat.'

'Yeah, man, the stage has rubber or something under the floor so it gives.'

Suddenly I saw a commotion over by the recording truck. Phil, who was supposed to be producing the recording inside the truck, had come out. He was a bit worse for wear and started arguing with some of the Secret Service guys. He told one to go fuck himself and then tried to punch him. A melee ensued between the security guys, the New York cops, and Claude Hayn and his Elephant's Memory roadies, who were trying to protect Phil. I pushed my way into the middle of it, dragged Phil out, and for his protection, shoved him on stage with John and Yoko, Stevie Wonder, Roberta Flack, Sha Na Na, Melanie, the Elephant's Memory, and a gaggle of other stars. Phil staggered, spun, and settled at a free keyboard.

A few minutes later I was standing backstage with an old friend, photographer Guy Cross. He said, 'This is incredible, Danny, you're doing an awful lot of work for them. Producing, record covers, organising these events . . . '

'Don't kid yourself, Guy. In the end, I'm just John's butler.'

A Spanish Vacation and a Shoot-out in Huston

Following the One to One Concert I had a clear sense that things had changed. John and Yoko had an unease about them that seemed to be a result of the trials they had gone through with the Nixon administration compounded by the battle to see Kyoko. I think they were tired and somewhat disillusioned. They had gone through so much in the year since they left Tittenhurst with so many dreams and aspirations. I was getting tired of my 'butler role' and the constant running back and forth between London and New York. I had used the safety of Ascot to kick heroin and was ready to get back to my own work. I wasn't a creature of the rock and roll world and I was losing my creative compass.

During September of 1972, we went on vacation to Jill's parents' home in Spain. They had a little place just off the beach in Altea, on the Costa Blanca. It was white stucco and bathed in vibrant sunlight. Hedges of red geraniums surrounded it. I needed the break.

John and Yoko said they would help me if I wanted to make a film. I wondered if they really meant it. As I was drawn more and more into their world, I got the feeling that the time would come when I would be pushed aside. John and Yoko used people up and when they had finished with them, gave them some money, helped them with a project, and sent someone like me with the news that the relationship was over.

I decided to get a script together and go for it. For a long time I had wanted to make a movie of Alex Trocchi's novel, *Cain's Book*. It was a dark tale of a Scots writer working and writing on a barge in New York harbour while using heroin. It had become a Beat classic and would make a perfect first feature. It was time to work on my own projects again.

In Spain, Jill and the family sat on the patio in the sun while inside I set up a spot to work on my treatment. Through the open window, I could hear the murmur of their voices and smell the sea. The work was flowing. All the creative energy that had accumulated while working on John and Yoko's projects was released and I finished the treatment during the week we spent there.

Back in London, I sent the treatment to Alex and as soon as he had read it I went up to his flat in Kensington to discuss it with him. I sat on his couch waiting nervously for his reaction.

'I think it's really grand Dan, with a wee bit of work we can have a fine screenplay.' Alex stood by the window with my treatment in his hands, the sun shining on his craggy features.

We agreed to start writing the script immediately and he set up a meeting with his agent the following week to discuss an option.

Excited, I told Yoko the news and she said she wanted to see the finished script.

On October 24, 1972, Alex and I signed an option deal for *Cain's Book*. It gave me the right to make a film of the book. I had until December 20th to make the first payment and until June 19th 1974 to complete the film. Alex and I finished the script and I gave a copy to Yoko and John.

During this same period the situation with Kyoko was coming to a head. Tony had surfaced in Houston and negotiations were taking place for Kyoko to visit Yoko.

'Dan, we are arranging for Kyoko to come up to New York to visit Yoko,' John explained to me as we talked in the bedroom at Bank Street.

'You're the perfect person to bring her back since Kyoko knows you and would be comfortable travelling with you,' said Yoko.

Yoko could make things sound so simple. I knew Tony, and I didn't trust him. I also didn't want to be involved any further in this dispute.

But I still wanted to help. It would be wonderful if Yoko could start seeing Kyoko again and a working relationship with Tony could be established.

I flew down to Houston where Tony was living. A court hearing was called to set up the visit. Something about it made me nervous. I didn't trust Tony. As I walked past him in the courtroom, he looked up at me with a strange smile and tried to hand me a folded-up piece of paper. I wouldn't take it. Once I was seated, his lawyer approached the bench and spoke with the judge who then turned and gave me a stern look. The judge called me up to the bench and, glaring right at me, said, 'Mr Cox's attorney tells me you are a drug addict.'

The room started to spin and I realised I'd been set up. My heart dropped at the prospect of a Texas jail. Looking at the judge over a Bible held upright by a pair of bronze praying hands, I fought to regain my composure. 'Well, your Honour,' I said, 'the drugs were all on prescription. Mr Cox uses drugs, too.'

Fixing me with a piercing stare he said, 'Young man, if I were you I'd turn around and leave this courtroom while you still can.'

As I turned and walked swiftly to the door, I heard him throwing Tony out as well.

The attorneys and I rushed around to the courthouse to get papers to serve Tony to keep him in Houston. Papers in hand, the attorneys, a security guy and I went to Melinda's family home. She was Tony's friend and we had heard they were staying there. We sat in a car in front of their house for several hours. There was no sign of them.

'Maybe one of us should go up and knock on the door.' I suggested.

'Do you want to borrow my gun?' asked the guy we had brought along to serve the papers.

'This is crazy, what am I doing here? I've got to get out of Texas,' I said to myself.

Tony, Kyoko, and Melinda had left the house. I was sure we

would never see them again. They would go into hiding among Tony's Jesus freak friends.

Just about everything to do with John and Yoko had become a big drag. I hated being so involved in Tony and Yoko's private business. The only positive aspect of my position was the possibility of making *Cain's Book*. I was tired of playing the part of John's errand boy.

Yoko Invests in Me (and *Cain's Book*)

It was December 20, 1972 and had just got off the phone with Yoko. I let out a shout and literally jumped in the air. She had read the script of *Cain's Book* and really liked it. She had agreed to help me produce the film. Her company, Ono Music, would own a percentage of the gross profits. She would advance me the money to secure the option with Alex and I could use the facilities of Joko Films in London and New York. We were planning to go right into pre-production, scouting locations and casting. It was a big step for me – I was finally going to produce and direct a feature film. I was finally doing my own work again.

On February 5, 1973 the contract with Ono Music was signed by both Yoko and myself. She gave me a check for $5,000 dollars to get the project into pre-production. We planned to shoot in September.

As spring approached, things moved quickly. I put together a great cast. Alex wanted the hero of the picture, Joe Necchi, to be played by a fine young actor named Keith Baxter. Keith had done a lot of film and TV, but was best known for his stage work playing Milo Tindle in *Sleuth* at St Martin's Theatre in London and at the Music Box on Broadway.

For Joe Necchi's eccentric father, we were talking with the great character actor Donald Pleasance.

Marianne Faithful sat across a table from me at Prunier's, just down St James from the Apple office. We were eating oysters.

'You'll be great, Marianne; you've got such a wonderful, fragile beauty.' I wanted her to play Joe's ex-wife Moira in *Cain's Book*.

'Do you really think I'll be good in it?'

'You'll be wonderful.'

As we ate our oysters, I looked at her across the table. I could see how much she had changed in the few years since that dinner when Paul showed up with the grass. The fresh-faced young girl just out of convent school had changed into a sad and worldly woman. Booze, dope, and the time she spent with Mick Jagger had taken its toll.

I was caught up in the work of getting *Cain's Book* into production as well as keeping up with John and Yoko's needs. I began to get careless.

'For Christ's sake, Alex, you know I can't use smack again.'

'A wee bit can't hurt you, Dan. I've some of that lovely China White heroin, it's the Tiger brand,' he said to me. It was a clear morning and we were sitting in his fourth floor flat high above Kensington going over the script.

Working on *Cain's Book* with him had meant that we were spending more and more time together. It was damn hard being around an active junky and not using. My dabbling with coke around the Apple office had opened the door a crack and I had a sinking feeling in my stomach.

'Well, I guess one shot won't hurt, but I'll be damned if I'll use it regularly again.' I could feel my head start to spin and my throat felt dry.

We both shot some of the China White and as the cloud of warmth filled my body, I was scared by the feeling of intense relief that came over me. It was as though I'd been holding my breath for two years and now I had finally taken one. I thought of something Bill Burroughs said – 'Anything that makes you feel that good, has to be illegal.'

Did I get involved with *Cain's Book* so that I could be around heroin again? At the time, I would have vehemently denied it and blamed Alex or the drag that the John and Yoko gig had become. Now in sobriety, I know that is exactly why I did it. We addicts are our own worst enemies. We can never let our guard down. As the old AA saying goes – while we are sleeping our disease is doing push-ups in the corner. Thinking back, in my insanity I believed that I had a good reason to use again. What a fucking idiot I was; a new baby, directing my first feature and I was sticking a needle in my arm!

Through Alex, I met a pretty young girl named Alice Ormsby-Gore. Alice was the daughter of Lord Harlech, a Conservative Member of Parliament, who had been the Ambassador to the United States in the early sixties. She had a skinny Pre-Raphaelite look about her. She was very young and would be just right for the part of the peg-legged gamin that Joe Necchi falls for. Alice lived with Eric Clapton at his estate, Hurtwood Edge.

'I really want to be in *Cain's Book*. Alex thinks I'd be perfect,' she said to me. She really was attractive and had a wonderful vulnerability about her.

'Well, you certainly look right and aside from the English accent, your manner is perfect for the part.'

Alice was a heroin addict and took care of Eric's habit by buying the heroin for him. Rock stars with habits always need someone like Alice or me to buy the drugs for them. She later died of an overdose.

'Eric would love to do the music for *Cain's Book*,' she said.

I was thinking of a jazz background, but Eric's music, with its bluesy intimacy, would be just right.

'I think we could work something out,' I said, trying not to sound too excited.

One evening Alex and I went down to meet with Eric at Hurtwood Edge. We wanted to talk about the music. Alice met us at the door and took us in to a large room and sat us down. Alex gave her some heroin for her and Eric and she disappeared upstairs.

Guitars, upright on their floor stands, filled one side of the large room we were sitting in.

'Man, will you look at all the guitars,' I said to Alex.

'How many do you think there are?' he asked.

'Twenty or thirty, I'd said.'

'Hi, Dan, Alex.' Eric and Alice came in and sat down.

We discussed their participation in the film and what we had scheduled. As we talked, I couldn't help thinking how much older we had all become in such a short time. In the three years since I first met Eric on the flight to the Toronto Rock and Roll Revival, he had lost his boyish quality. Heroin takes a terrible toll and addicts can decline very rapidly. I was using it again in bits. Working with Alex had proven to be very hazardous.

Having made all of our arrangements, we said good night and Alex and I drove back to London.

It was late May 1973 and Steve Gebhardt and I were standing in front of the Rolling Stones recording studio waiting for them to show up, Bob Fries had already gone inside. We were going to see a screening of a new Reggae Film called *The Harder They Come*. Steve was in town working on a TV version of *Imagine* and Bob was over-dubbing some Mick Taylor bits in the Stones film here at Olympic Studios.

'Steve, everything is working out great – all of John and Yoko's films, *Cain's Book*, the Stones Film. We are really busy.' I said to him.

'I wish they were making more money,' he said. 'Hey, give me a toke of that thing.'

Barnes is a posh suburb just south of London on the Thames. It was almost 9:00 pm and, London being so far north, the sun hadn't set yet. We were standing looking at the river and smoking a joint and discussing all the projects that we were doing with Joko Films.

Suddenly we heard the high-pitched whine of a high-performance engine and a red Ferrari came speeding up to the studio. It came right at us, then stopped just inches from where we were cowering.

'Hey, how're ya doing? Come on in,' said Keith Richard, laughing as he and a guy I knew as Prince Stash got out of the Ferrari. Keith waved us toward the entrance of the studio and we followed him in.

Olympic was a large studio with plenty of room for us all inside. Mick arrived a bit later. A fellow who looked like a Rasta dressed in a long African robe arrived and handed some film cans to the projectionist.

The film was really great with wonderful Jamaican music. Afterwards, we discussed the Stones film with Mick and Keith. That night as Steve and I drove back into London we looked at each other and smiled. Things were really going great. They couldn't be better.

Dear John

No! I was not Prince Hamlet, nor was meant to be;
Am an attendant lord, one that will do
To swell a progress, start a scene or two,
Advise the prince; no doubt, an easy tool,
Deferential, glad to be of use,
Politic, cautious, and meticulous;
Full of high sentence, but a bit obtuse;
At times, indeed, almost ridiculous –
Almost, at times, the Fool.

The Love Song of J. Alfred Prufrock
T. S. Eliot

John and Yoko had bought a large apartment in the Dakota, a massive, fortress-like building at the corner of 72nd Street and Central Park West. They traded the cramped two-room dive on Bank Street for a spacious complex for the rich. Bank Street looked onto the back of another building; the Dakota had great windows looking directly onto Central Park with the city spread out beyond. Instead of a guy rebuilding a motorcycle in front of the tiny Bank Street apartment, there was a large gated entry-way with a uniformed doorman.

It was May 30, 1973 and I was talking to Yoko on the phone. She said that they wanted to take a break from film-making, recording, and political activity. They wanted to concentrate on resolving John's immigration problems and the search for Kyoko. She said they were going to stay in New York and they didn't need Tittenhurst any more. They wanted me to stay in England to look after their interests there. And then, just like that, she told me they were closing down Joko Films and she was withdrawing her support of *Cain's Book*. As I listened to her on the other end of the phone, my head was spinning and my stomach felt like I was in an elevator in free fall. Without her backing and the resources of Joko, the project would fall apart.

I told Yoko that if we had to leave Ascot and I had to live in England, I was quitting. I told her that I only signed on for the films and projects, and if that was over, I didn't want to sit in the Apple office in London, pushing paper around and pretending to work.

John came on the phone and we started to argue.

'You and Jill stay in England and I'll take care of you for life,' he said.

'I can't do it, John. I only came along for the ride.'

'I'll buy you and Jill a house outside of London.'

'Thanks for the offer, John, but I can't do it. I'm leaving.'

'You can't leave, Dan. You know too much,' he said.

So it had come to this – after all we had been through, they didn't even trust me. I was furious and, with my head still spinning, I said, 'John, I'll make it easy for you. Fuck you!'

I hung up the phone and ordered first-class plane tickets to take me and the family back to the States.

A day later, as Jill, Sacha, Mischa, and I settled on the plane for Boston, Jill looked at me and said, 'Dan, what are we going to do now?'

Across the Universe

'I really don't want to be here.' I thought to myself. It was February 1974 and I was sitting in a modern waiting room of a large law firm in a glass tower high above 6th Avenue in New York. I had gotten away from this whole crazy world of rock and roll, and I liked it much better that way. Away from London I had stopped my heroin use and made the commitment to stay away from it and to slowly taper off the Methadone. As part of my new regime I had returned to the American Mime Theatre and was getting back in shape.

I was nervous about meeting with a group of attorneys regarding a lawsuit John Lennon had against Allen Klein. The music business seemed to always be enmeshed in litigations and I had gotten out of all that. I stayed in touch with Yoko and John through Jill who was helping Yoko out with day-to-day things, but after ten years I was once again a mime performer and teacher and that's where I belonged.

'Go right in, Mr Richter, they are ready for you.'

As I entered a large glassed-walled conference room I heard a familiar voice singing.

> 'Oh Danny boy, the pipes, the pipes are calling
> From glen to glen, and down the mountain side.
> The summer's gone, and all the flowers are dying . . . '

'Oh my God,' I thought. 'It's John!'

What a great surprise. I couldn't help smiling as I listened to him singing. He was sitting at the end of a long conference table with light flowing in from the floor-to-ceiling windows behind him.

There was a gaggle of about twenty attorneys around the table. John had that familiar quirky smile on his face, and we were both pleased to see each other. I slide into a seat they had waiting for me at the other end of the long table. It was a relief to see him looking so well.

I was worried about him. A few months before, he left the security of Yoko and the Dakota to be with May Pang. Sensing that he was becoming restless in their relationship, Yoko encouraged May to be open to his advances. Poor May was very uncomfortable with the suggestion, but when Yoko had a plan, it usually went her way. Yoko knew that with John seeing May, she had some control over his dalliance. She also thought it would make him realise how much he needed her. Away from Yoko, John had experienced a certain freedom. He and May had fun together, they loved to talk about rock and roll and he could record and see friends without Yoko controlling everything. But with this freedom, John's wild self-destructive side emerged. After a few drinks he could become wild and violent. Years before, on the evening of Paul McCartney's twenty-first birthday, John had almost killed someone. Like many of us who have drinking problems, he found both a refuge and a safer release in drugs. Without Yoko's direction, he was very vulnerable and began to drink too much.

It was appropriate to see John surrounded by lawyers. People had a romanticised view of the very rich and famous and particularly of rock stars. One doesn't think of Mick Jagger as being a consummate businessman who studied at the London School of Economics. He developed complex business models for the Stones' tours that maximised revenues while containing expenses and tax liabilities across multiple countries. At this point in his life John was an extremely rich man, worth hundreds of millions of dollars. The value of his share of the publishing rights of the Beatles songs was staggering, not to mention the rights to his future works. Publishing rights dominate the music business and become very convoluted with sync rights, mechanical rights, and many other complicated aspects of musical intellectual property. Owning and controlling these rights was at the core of the music business. All the battles and lawsuits that plague the business flow from this central fact. That was why we were sitting around that table.

Placed in an imposing row down the centre of the conference table were storage files full of documents. A few days before, Jane Parva, a young, good-looking attorney in a pin-striped suit, had approached me on John's behalf to peruse them. She wanted to see if there was anything in them that would help John in a lawsuit against his one-time friend and manager Allen Klein. Not wanting to stick my head in the lion's mouth, I asked to be indemnified with a hold harmless. The last thing I wanted was to be dragged into a lawsuit between John and Allen. Jane arrived at my apartment in the Chelsea Hotel with the boxes and a legal letter. I couldn't help smiling as I read ' . . . between everyone and everything, everywhere, forever and for all time, including, without limitation . . . ' I accepted and signed the letter, and Jane left the boxes stacked in the middle of my sitting room. They sat there like a row of tombstones. I knew they would be full of the corpses of events that would arise, ghostlike, when I opened them. Since leaving the chaos of the rock and roll world, I had spent almost two years putting some semblance of sanity back into my life. Such a lovely day, what had I got myself into?

Three days later, on the morning of the meeting, a limo picked me up for a conference with John's attorneys.

'Dan, these people want to know if you think there is anything here I can use in the suit with Allen.' John indicated the row of boxes and the dark suits on either side of the table. We both knew that there was probably little that John's attorneys could use, but with so much at stake, every stone had to be turned even if the process was costly, tiring, and a dreadful bore.

'I can't find anything, John. If Allen had done something that you could use against him, I can't imagine him leaving it around,' I said.

The attorneys, wanting to be as thorough as possible, asked me a few questions and we discussed what I had read. Then, having done his duty, John looked at one of the senior attorneys and asked, 'Is there an empty office we can use for a few minutes?'

'Of course, Mr Lennon, let me have someone show you.' One of the younger attorneys jumped up and we were ushered into a nearby office.

As the door closed, we looked at each other, there was an awkward pause, then the veneer of a major star faded from John's face and we made an awkward attempt at a hug.

'Are you OK, Dan? How are Jill and the kids?'

'We are doing great. I'm back at the American Mime Theatre for a year on a Rockefeller grant. I've managed to stay off heroin and I'm performing and helping write a new mime play. It's great to perform again.'

As we talked, I looked at the gangly, awkward, smiling old friend, trapped forever in the straitjacket of the Beatles' John Lennon. I thought back on all we had been through together. The struggle with heroin, the 'kidnapping' of Kyoko in Majorca, all the films and recordings we made.

'You've got one of those plain buttons?'

He had noticed a small white button I was wearing. He had designed it for his first exhibition, *You Are Here* in July 1968 at the Robert Fraser Gallery, London. The button was a classic Yokoesque conceptual art statement. It was completely blank.

'I don't have one; I thought they were all gone,' he said.

'Take it.' I removed the button and handed it to him.

'Do you have any more?' he asked, hesitating.

'It doesn't matter, John, you created it. It's from your first show, you should have it.'

'Thanks, mate. Thanks a lot. I guess we should go back in. You know I'm paying these suits by the hour?'

As we left the office, John metamorphosed back into John Lennon. He paused to brush his fingers through his hair, something I had seen him do a thousand times before. We each went back to our seats around the table. My part of the meeting was over. As I left, the last image I had of him was sitting at the end of that long conference table surrounded by attorneys, with light streaming out behind him.

I never saw John again.

My Passport Stamps (1969–73)

Here is a log of my passport stamps from 1969 to 1973 covering the period that I was with Yoko and John. While the stamps represent most of the trips I took, there were many trips that were not represented. Some of the stamps were illegible. Other times in New York ABKO arranged for customs to perform a 'spot check' on me and then whisked me to the limo. Often the passport was simply not stamped by customs.

1969

Thursday, May 1, 1969 Jill & Sacha	Trip to Ptown	London	Embarked
Wednesday, July 2, 1969		London	Arrived
Saturday, September 13, 1969 John & Yoko, Jill, Eric Clapton, Alan White	Toronto R&R	London	Embarked
Monday, September 15, 1969	London	Arrived	
Tuesday, November 4, 1969 – Munich Arriflex		London	Embarked
Tuesday, November 4, 1969	London	Arrived	

1970

Tuesday, October 6, 1970 John's birthday search	S of France	London	Embarked
Thursday, October 8, 1970		London	Arrived
Monday, November 16, 1970	New York	London	Embarked
Tuesday, November 17, 1970	New York	Arrived	
Friday, November 20, 1970	London	Arrived	
Thursday, December 03, 1970	New York	London	Embarked

Thursday, December 03, 1970	J&Y Film Festival		
		New York	Arrived
Monday, December 21, 1970		London	Arrived

1971

Thursday, January 7, 1971		London	Embarked
Friday, January 8, 1971		London	Arrived
Sunday, April 18, 1971 John & Yoko	Z Charnoe & Palma	Gatwick	Embarked
Sunday, April 18, 1971		Bordeaux	Arrived
Sunday, April 18, 1971		Bordeaux	Arrived
Monday, April 19, 1971		Merignac	
Monday, April 19, 1971		Palma	Arrived
Wednesday, April 21, 1971		Palma	Embarked
Wednesday, April 21, 1971		London	Arrived
Thursday, April 22, 1971 John & Yoko	'Kidnapping'	London	Embarked
Sunday, April 25, 1971		London	Arrived
Friday, May 14, 1971 John & Yoko	Cannes Fortnight of the Directors	London	Embarked
Friday, May 14, 1971		Nice	Arrived
Monday, May 17, 1971		Nice	Embarked
Monday, May 17, 1971		London	Arrived
Wednesday, May 19, 1971	Cannes	London	Embarked
Wednesday, May 19, 1971		Nice	Arrived
Saturday, May 22, 1971		Nice	Embarked
Saturday, May 22, 1971		London	Arrived
Tuesday, June 01, 1971	Palma Judge	London	Embarked
Wednesday, June 07, 1971	Marrakech	Casablanca	Arrived

Monday, June 12, 1971		Marrakech	Embarked
Sunday, June 13, 1971		London	Arrived
Thursday, June 17, 1971		New York	Arrived
Saturday, July 03, 1971		London	Arrived
Monday, July 26, 1971 John & Yoko	Custody St Thomas	London	Embarked
Wednesday, July 26, 1971		Antigua	Arrived
Saturday, July 31, 1971	NY Bangladesh	London	Arrived
Saturday, November 27, 1971	Attica Benefit at the Apollo	London	Embarked
Friday, December 24, 1971		London	Arrived

1972

Monday, January 31, 1972 – NY		London	Embarked
Thursday, February 17, 1972		London	Arrived
Tuesday, March 14, 1972	Switzerland?	London	Embarked
Monday, March 20, 1972	NY	London	Embarked
Tuesday, March 28, 1972		New York	Arrived
Thursday, April 13, 1972		London	Arrived
Thursday, May 04, 1972	Cannes #2	London	Embarked
Thursday, May 04, 1972	Nice	Arrived	
Tuesday, May 09, 1972	NY	London	Arrived
Tuesday, May 23, 1972	NY	London	Embarked
Wednesday, June 21, 1972		London	Arrived
Saturday, August 12, 1972	NY	London	Embarked
?	No stamp	London	Arrived
Monday, August 21, 1972 – One to One Concert		London	Embarked
Sunday, September 03, 1972		London	Arrived

Monday, September 11, 1972	Altea	London	Embarked
Monday, September 11, 1972		Barcelona	Arrived
Wednesday, September 27, 1972		London	Arrived
Tuesday, October 10, 1972	NY	London	Embarked
Sunday, October 22, 1972		London	Arrived
Wednesday, November 15, 1972	NY	London	Embarked
Friday, December 01, 1972		London	Arrived

1973

Thursday, May 31, 1973 Dan, Jill, Sacha, & Mischa	Return to the US	London	Embarked
Thursday, May 31, 1973		Boston	Arrived

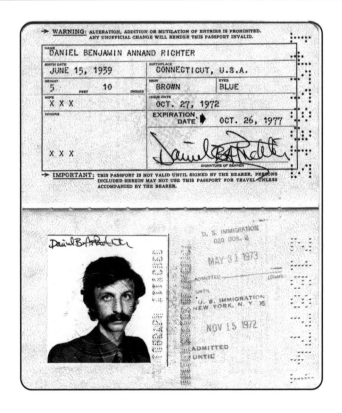

231

Acknowledgements

A lot of people helped me with this memoir and I want to thank them all. I would like to give special thanks to Jill Richter who helped me with the edit and to Yoko Ono for being Yoko.